FIFTY SHADES OF IKEA

ROBIN SEGAL

COPYRIGHT © 2014, Robin Segal

ISBN 978-1-935139-22-5

Murray Hill Books, LLC
www.murrayhillbooks.com

ACKNOWLEDGEMENTS

I would like to thank all those who inspired me to write this book: the six TARVA beds, eleven JANSJO lamps, eight NESNA bedside tables, my five by five EXPEDIT shelf with white finish, and of course my first BILLY who never failed me.

Thanks to my friend Sam, who drove over to help me lift my EXPEDIT off the floor where I had assembled it myself in three hours instead of with a friend in one. Thanks also to IKEA's PATRULL bandages 50 pack, with pink and orange cartoons of cats or bears with wounds and doctor bags on them, and instructions in twenty-five languages, which protected my fingers, blistered from thousands of turns of my trusty hex keys in order to assemble the six beds and eight tables and eleven lamps in three days.

Thank you to IKEA's meatballs, which kept me coming back to eat, and then of course to shop, in order to justify driving ten kilometers to eat meatballs and potatoes. Thank you to the lady working the hot food line who, seeing that approximately six French fries fell off the plate as she placed them, followed my gaze, retrieved the fallen fries, and placed them once again on the plate. Thank you also to IKEA's giant glazed cinnamon bun & bottomless coffee one dollar special (weekdays 2 to 5 PM,) which lured me in to shop many times and which made me happy. And who can argue with happiness.

Contents

INTRODUCTION

Hello and welcome to my book, FIFTY SHADES OF IKEA.
When FIFTY SHADES OF GREY became popular, I was oblivi-
ous to it. I was selling a house, buying a house, and moving,
and I simply missed the whole phenomenon. It was only when
I learned that the book is the fastest selling book in human history that I took any interest in what it was even about. There
is so much fine writing, so many good stories, so much to read
that connects us to writers' humanity that unites us as a species.
The fact that a not very well written book that glorifies abusive
relationships is flying off the shelves faster than any other book
ever has, is sad.

When I learned what FIFTY SHADES OF GREY was all about,
I was spending a lot of time at IKEA, furnishing a large house
for a quick rental. One day, while pushing my shopping cart
through IKEA's lighting department, I thought it would be
funny to write fifty essays about fifty IKEA lamp shades, window shades, or shades of color. Before I knew it, I had started
listing writing genres, musing that if I could identify fifty genres,
I could write about fifty shades in fifty genres. I soon listed fifty
genres, including poetry, but had to relax my definition of *shade*
to the more general *aspect*. And, admittedly, I relax my definition
of *genre* to include warning labels and recipes.

Sixteen of the fifty sections of this book are in verse. Like most
people, until recently I did not know a villanelle from a terza
rima. Recognizing that it might be interesting to know something about the fifty written genres I used, I added a glossary of
genres at the end.

SONNET

When I first took you home to stay with me
I knew that you and I would get along
Although you were so plain, still I could see
That you were handsome, capable and strong

Day after day, you stayed, you did not budge
You always gave support, and shone your light
Although I was a sloth, you did not judge
And if I slept, you stayed with me all night

Like each of us you've had your spills and dips
So through the years you've grown a little rough
And silently, you even suffered chips
Your smooth veneer shines through though, ever tough

Tis with great fondness I on you look back
My trusted, loyal, cheap side table, LACK.

LEGEND

It is said that during his brief reign from 1155 to 1160, King Eric IX of Sweden went to holy Christian battle in the first Swedish Crusade of 1157. King Eric looked up, legend holds, and saw a cross of gold on the blue sky. Obviously a sign from God, King Eric adopted the gold cross on blue as Sweden's flag. Although sky blue is much lighter than Swedish-flag-blue, it can be assumed that a darker blue was more practical against the pale blue sky, since the flag was flown on ships and seen against the sky for over a thousand years, before being a more familiar sight against the Swedish landscape. King Eric, being detail-oriented, and having a keen eye for design, specified Pantone 109 (yellow) and Pantone 293 (blue), in records stored faithfully to this day in the Swedish Royal Design Archives.

King Eric came to be considered a saint. He has a feast day, which is May 18, although he was never canonized by the Vatican. IKEA corporate legend holds that Eric's formal denial of saint status inspired IKEA to create some votive style candles, MARTIR, ($14.99/four pack, Marketplace.) Instead of real flames, MARTIR candle lights would use photovoltaic-powered plastic LED "flames," more realistically, and poetically, reflecting the sunlight of the blue sky seen by King Eric. Sadly, this IKEA product remains on the drawing board.

Legend also holds that King Eric was beheaded in battle, and where his head fell to earth, a fountain spontaneously sprang up. This chapter of the legend has not, to date, inspired any IKEA products.

While the gold cross on blue sky is the legendary basis for IKEA's blue and golden yellow corporate colors, blue and gold were not always IKEA's colors. IKEA's original logo was red and white, resembling a red wax seal (signifying quality and approval.) The logo was circular, but with small lines around the circle, with white lettering, "Ikéa." Eventually this logo became an oval, still with lines or petals around the edge, although the shape looked more like a puffy cloud. The lettering became more modern.

The logo was further streamlined, becoming a simple oval with just the four letters IKEA, no accent above the E. The red and white color scheme continued to be used, but the yellow and blue color scheme also appeared.

An inquisitive mind might ask, why red and white? For the answer to this question, we return to the time of the Crusades. Less than one hundred years after King Eric saw the gold cross on the blue sky, the neighboring Danish army of the righteous were themselves on a holy crusade in Estonia. Things were not going well, and a priest on site was praying for military strength. Just when he was about to give up, a red and white flag fell right out of the sky. By some accounts, this flag was a "lamb-skin banner." There is evidence that the Danes were assisted by the Knights Hospitalier from Malta. Their banner, the red and white Maltese cross, may have been the source of the Danish red and white flag.

Denmark was a much larger country before the twentieth century. The southern part of Sweden, called Scania, was Danish territory for most of civilized history. Ingvar Kamprad was born in the province of Småland, just a few meters from the border of Scania. The Danish language, not the Swedish language, was spoken in this part of Sweden until about one hundred years before Ingvar's birth. Scania was the seat of the Danish reformation, and some say culturally more Danish than Swedish, even to this day.

IKEA's corporate headquarters moved from Sweden to Denmark in 1975. Just a few years after that, the company's current logo appeared… in red and white. Just a few years later, the logo colors shifted to yellow and blue and not long after that, IKEA corporate headquarters were moved to the Netherlands.

ANTHEM

Your meatballs, your flatpacks, your Småland playroom
Your most alluring color catalog
Your pictorial assembly instructions
We always keep a hex key in our pockets
We always keep a hex key in our pockets

Your blue and your yellow of global renown
Your coffee and cinnamon bun special!
Around the world, the many people love you
We always keep a hex key in our pockets
We always keep a hex key in our pockets

Swedish National Anthem:

Du gamla, Du fria, Du fjällhöga nord
Du tysta, Du glädjerika sköna!
Jag hälsar Dig, vänaste land uppå jord
Din sol, Din himmel, Dina ängder gröna
Din sol, Din himmel, Dina ängder gröna

You free, ancient country, you high mountained north
Thou quiet, thou joyful beauty!
We greet you as loveliest land upon earth
Your shining sun, your sky, your pastures green
Your shining sun, your sky, your pastures green

COMPLAINT

Several years ago, I bought a dehumidifier online, through
Amazon.com. Four years later, there was a giant product recall,
due to several incidences of spontaneous combustion. Amazon
emailed me to let me know which website to visit for specific
information. My dehumidifier was on the recall list, so I filled
out the online form, received a prepaid envelope in the mail,
and as instructed, mailed in the cord and some labels. A couple
of months later, I received a full refund. I am still amazed that
Amazon keeps records in such a way that this was even possible,
let alone successful.

IKEA issued this product recall in 2010: "If you have an IKEA
Roller Blind, without an attached tension device, Roman Blind
or Roll-Up Blind, please bring it back to your local IKEA for a
full refund. IKEA has decided to make a proactive, precautionary recall; the action is performed in collaboration with the US
Consumer Safety Commission. If installed incorrectly, cords
and looped bead chains could present a strangulation hazard to
young children." I had some of those roll-up blinds, but it was
only this year that I happened to find this recall, despite numer-
ous visits to and emails from IKEA. Why didn't IKEA try harder
to reach out to me? Somebody could have called. The Swedes
keep excellent records- why can't IKEA do the same? I feel un-
important, unloved, anonymous.

PRODUCT RECALL

If you have an IKEA DANSA (Disco ball with LED light, Children's department,) please bring it back to your local IKEA for a full refund. IKEA has decided to make a proactive, precautionary recall; the action is performed in collaboration with the US National Endowment for the Arts. If installed correctly, young children could develop a taste for disco music, including soaring reverberating vocals, prominent syncopated electric bass line, and chronic repetition into adulthood of phrases such as "Le Freak, c'est chic."

QUATRAIN

It looks so stunning in the showroom
T'would make my home a grand château
I realize sadly I have no room
In my tiny studio

FORMULA

The formula for computing the surface area of a lamp shade, called the frustum of a hollow cone, in order to cover the lamp shade in fabric:

The lateral surface area for a complete cone is:

A = pi*R*S where R is the radius and S is the slant height of the whole cone.

For the frustum, we will subtract the area of the cut-off cone (whose slant height is S-s) from the whole:

A = pi*R*S - pi*r*(S-s)
= pi*(RS - rS + rs)
= pi*((R-r)S + rs)

By similar triangles, we can write:
R/S = r/(S-s)

Solving for S,
R(S-s) = rS
RS - Rs = rS
RS - rS = Rs
(R-r)S = Rs
S = Rs /R-r

Now the area is
A = pi ((R-r)*rs/(R-r)+rs)
 = pi (Rs + rs)
 = pi(R+r)s

 That is how much fabric you need, plus ¼" all around for seams.

D.I.Y. INSTRUCTIONS

While IKEA sells many lamp shades, most are either white or beige. Sometimes they have some kind of interesting interior color or embroidery, but most are neutral territory. IKEA fabrics, on the other hand, are wild and terrific. Let's say you want to buy some bed linens, and then cover a lamp shade with matching fabric from the fabric department. Great idea! But you would need to know how much fabric to buy. Luckily, the people in the mathematics department have provided us with a handy formula for figuring this out exactly.

Before you start, note that a lamp shade is a giant cone minus a small dunce cap sliced off the top. OK, we're ready. Those of you who are pretty mathy can take a peek at the previous section of this book and shortcut these instructions right over to your craft table! For the rest of us who doodled in the margins during algebra, read on.

(1) Measure the diameter of the top of your lamp shade and the diameter of the bottom of your lamp shade. Divide each in half to get the radii. (2) Measure the height of the lamp shade = h. (3) Now, to derive the sloped side that makes a right angle triangle, you need to follow these simple steps: (a) use the Pythagorean theorem to find the sloped side of the lamp shade plus the sloped side of the missing dunce cap on top: the square of the hypotenuse (the side opposite the right angle) is equal to the sum of the squares of the other two sides. In other words, h squared plus r squared = square of the sloped side, (to find the height of the lamp shade plus dunce cap, you need to extend the sloped side until it meets the horizontal center of the lamp shade,) then (b) repeat (a) for only the dunce cap, and (c) subtract the dunce cap from the imaginary cone to find the squared length of the sloped side of the lamp shade. Then, of course,

take the square root of that. Alternatively, ignore this paragraph up to here and then: measure the lamp shade with a ruler.

Now that you have the sloped height of the lamp shade, you still have to figure out the area of the awkward rectangle that looks like it has been bent into a smile. (The longest width is equal to the circumference of the bottom edge of the lamp shade. Circumference is 2*pi*r. Area is length * width.) You also have to figure out how to place the fabric so that the pattern looks good. The last thing you want is to save two dollars and cover a lamp shade in fabric that looks like it is slipping off, or is on sideways, or something like that. Calculating all of this is impossible, since it is entirely dependent on the repeat in the pattern, which usually comes at 3, 6, 9, or even every 27 inches. Horizontally and vertically. Clearly, Pythagoras lived before the invention of the repeat pattern.

Luckily, the people in the fabric department at IKEA have a shortcut for knowing how much fabric to cut AND for placing the fabric correctly on the lamp shade: (1) Take your lamp shade from the lighting department to the fabric department, (2) wrap your lamp shade in fabric, exactly the way you want it to look, (3) hand the whole thing to the fabric department person and ask him or her to cut you as much as you need plus half a yard.

FAIRY TALE

Once upon a time, there lived a family of three bears in a lovely birch veneer cabin in the forest. One day, the bears prepared some sweet porridge and went for a walk while their porridge cooled.

About this time, a girl named Goldilocks, who had been wandering through the same forest, came upon the Bears' cabin. The cabin smelled of sweet porridge, and although she knew it was wrong, she entered without permission.

Goldilocks took one look at the Papa bear's porridge bowl. Papa bear had served himself a triple serving of porridge in a large, deep glass serving dish with minimal surface area, so that it would take forever to cool. This TRYGG dish, mused Goldilocks, as she recognized the design, is misused as a dinner plate, particularly for soup. Moving along, Goldilocks observed that Mama bear had served herself a tiny drop of porridge on a glass FRODIG side plate, and had consumed it already, but had, surmised Goldilocks, accompanied Papa Bear and Baby Bear on their walk in the interest of family harmony. Goldilocks found Baby Bear's porridge in a 6" beige DINERA bowl ($2.00, or part of an 18-piece dinner set, $29.99). Baby Bear's porridge was just the right temperature. Finally, somebody who had chosen the appropriate portion size and plate. Although she knew it was wrong, Goldilocks ate Baby bear's porridge.

At this point in the story, you might be expecting Goldilocks to try out Papa Bear's swivel reclining brown leather VRETA armchair, Mama Bear's classic EKTORP armchair in MOBACKA beige and red stripes, and Baby Bear's white SUNDVIK children's rocking chair. You also might expect this exercise to continue with Goldilocks preferring Baby Bear's SULTAN HOL-

MSTA latex pillowtop spring mattress on his SVÄRTA bunk bed frame, her settling in to nap in Baby Bear's bed, and the bears discovering her when they in from their walk.

But that's not what happened. Once Goldilocks had analyzed the family members' dinnerware and portion preferences, she realized how one's relationship to eating has the potential to shape one's other choices, even a life's general trajectory. In addition, Goldilocks already felt guilty about trespassing and stealing the Bears' food, and knew she needed to dedicate her life to doing good. Goldilocks left the Bears' cabin, ran as fast as she could through the forest, and registered for an associate degree in nutritional counseling.

MYSTERY

It is a morning scene from practically anywhere on earth, IKEA co-workers filing in to the iconic blue and yellow big box store, banners flapping in the wind. Gathering in the restaurant for employee breakfast meeting, they fling coats and bags on the chairs and march across the empty dining room to the cafeteria line.

On this particular morning in IKEA Edinburgh, Oscar stood before the grill, scrambling eggs. Oscar was a kitchen co-worker. He almost never worked up at the line, but when he did have such an opportunity, he would make conversation with every single customer. This could be the reason he rarely had the opportunity. In any case, on this morning, Anna, who regularly worked the bread and toast station, had called in to the IKEA employee overnight answering service to describe her health status.

"I'm feeling off, not really well enough to drive to work, and heaven forbid anybody should catch what I might have picked up from my nephew Marcus, who is visiting from the United States, because you know what floats around in that re-circulated air on the planes, these days. I'm sure I will be fine by tomorrow. And I shouldn't say so, but today Marcus has gone back up to Inverness to spend some time exploring the grounds of the abandoned Northern County District Lunatic Asylum. He so loves its splendid hilltop site and parklike grounds. I do love Marcus, but he is young and energetic, and I need a day at home alone to regroup."

Anna loved to talk, and she could go on and on, but she had the discipline to move things along, never letting the restaurant line get too long. Willpower, Anna liked to say, was one of IKEA's core values. Anna reviewed the employee handbook once a week, and liked to spread its wisdom to new employees. Anna came to Scotland from Sweden when IKEA Edinburgh opened, over ten years earlier, and she fell in love with the city of Edinburgh, its people, the highlands, and probably its whisky as well. Whatever the reason, Anna remained at IKEA Edinburgh, was loved and valued by all, so IKEA Edinburgh was happy to keep her on for as long as she wished to stay.

Since Anna was staying home, Felicia, a seasoned IKEA co-worker, who normally scrambled the eggs, was called to the bread and toast station. With Oscar filling in at the grill, everything was under control. The morning meeting went smoothly, like most every day, and when the store opened to customers half an hour later, some restaurant co-workers were finishing up the breakfast preparation, and moving on, either to prepare the cold lunch plates for the display cooler or to fetch frozen entrees from the walk-in freezer.

Suddenly, a scream of terror was heard throughout the restaurant. Most screams of terror are sudden. It is hard to imagine how any sound could actually "lead up" to a scream of terror, since part of the experience of terror is surprise, and in fact, silence is the sound that makes the terror scream most chilling.

Naturally, everybody ran over to the walk-in freezer to see who had screamed and why. After it had been determined that nobody had been hurt, nothing stolen, and nothing broken, Felicia, the screamer, was led to a chair, calmed, and given a glass of water. The most senior restaurant manager asked Felicia what had upset her so. After her breathing had returned nearly to normal and she had stopped shivering, Felicia explained that when she entered the walk-in freezer to fetch some frozen fish, she saw, lying on the floor, motionless, a five by five, birch effect, fully assembled EXPEDIT shelving unit. Felicia broke down and sobbed, and it was several minutes and two cinnamon buns with extra glaze later that Felicia felt calm enough to reveal what she had seen that had filled her heart with dread. The EXPEDIT unit's twenty-five cubic storage compartments, continued Felicia, were filled with frozen lingonberry juice.

"Somebody at IKEA has wasted gallons and gallons of lingonberry juice, thereby violating IKEA's core value of cost-consciousness," Felicia whispered, clearly horrified by such an action. She looked up at the faces of the IKEA co-workers gathered around her, and began to cry again.

Felicia was sent home to rest. She was replaced in the kitchen by Engelbert Fischer an IKEA co-worker originally from Munich, with steelier nerves than Felicia, and confident enough to take on any position at any moment. A command center was set up for local law enforcement and store security personnel. The command center was really just a table situated very close to the beverage and condiment island. It was expected that this deranged crime, or juicy prank, or whatever it was, would take a long block of at least a few bakers dozen man-hours of detective work. These dedicated minds working around the clock to figure out and apprehend whoever had made twenty-five giant lingonberry popsicles would require plenty of coffee and cinnamon buns. Also, word of the prank, and the free coffee and pastry for those on the case, spread like wildfire among local law enforcement personnel. And, once the fire department "misheard" over the radio that something, anything, actually, at IKEA, was "spreading like wildfire," firefighters drove over as well to make sure everything was OK.

Aside from being overwhelmed by demand for cinnamon buns, and outnumbered by uniformed Edinburgh law enforcement officials, the IKEA kitchen was almost back to normal, thanks to Engelbert, Oscar, and the other capable IKEA co-workers. It was not long before Edinburgh Police Department Volunteer Special Constable Percy Clark called out, "Over here! In the freezer!" Edinburgh South Chief Constable Simon Seize (his father served in the French security detail under Louis XVI), rose from his command center BOJNE armchair ($99) and walked briskly to the walk-in freezer. Constable Seize was very proud of the volunteer Special Constables force. Its members were young, eager, and in considerably better physical condition than the older police force. When he arrived at the walk-in freezer, Constable Seize saw eight Volunteer Special Constables conducting a grid search on their hands and knees. Although he was only two yards from the freezer door, Volunteer Special Constable Percy Clark locked eyes with Edinburgh South Chief Constable Seize, and, as he had been trained, pointed to the floor, and yelled as though to somebody five hundreds yards away, "I! HAVE! FOUND! SOME! THING!"

The item Percy had found on the floor was a copper ring, slightly larger than a ring for a finger, nearly two inches in circumference and just over one inch deep. Attached to the ring was a rubber band, covered in a fabric sleeve. The evidence team was called over from the command station. Light meters were used, photographs taken, measurements notated on evidence cards, everything lifted with nitrile gloves and sealed in plastic bags, according to protocol. The ring and elastic object, in its evidence bag, was passed around the command station. Nobody knew what to make of it. All they did know for certain was that it did not belong in the walk-in freezer.

Engelbert Fischer approached the command center. His co-workers held their breath for they knew what to expect. Outside IKEA's royal blue walls, people did not appreciate Engelbert's enthusiasm, his self-confidence, his appetite for a challenge large or small, or unfortunately his lack of personal boundaries. To add to his general lust for life, Engelbert was very well rested, as he had just returned from a week's holiday in Mallorca with his extended German family. Engelbert's father had retired from his career as a scientist, and the family vacation was a big celebration. Engelbert had overdone it in the sun, fallen asleep a couple of times without sunblock. He radiated heat and redness, wore a loosely fitting IKEA uniform shirt, and rubbed cooling aloe gel on his normally pale neck several times a day.

"Where are we with this?" The police officers stared at Engelbert. The restaurant manager saw the scene from across the dining area and ran over, calling, "Engelbert, it's OK, the security people have this under control! They can handle it. Please return to your kitchen duties."

"Yes, right away," said Engelbert, smoothly. "Just trying to contribute my cleverness. My father is a scientist. Scientific method, in my blood, you know." Being unfamiliar with Engelbert's character, Edinburgh South Chief Constable Simon Seize was struck on the brain by a bolt of suspicion. Casually, he expressed appreciation for Engelbert's assistance and attitude, all the while calculating the young co-worker's actions, words and expressions. You do not get to be Edinburgh South Chief Constable by missing clues, thought Simon Seize. He smiled inwardly, for to have smiled outwardly would have been inappropriate.

Edinburgh South Chief Constable Simon Seize walked Engelbert back to the kitchen. There, he motioned to Oscar. Oscar spoke with Edinburgh South Chief Constable Simon Seize, telling him that only two weeks earlier, Engelbert had floated the idea of IKEA frozen treats, including lingonberry sorbet. Oscar remembered that Engelbert had been inspired by the Starbucks employee who invented the Frappuccino and whose life had changed forever. Edinburgh South Chief Constable Simon Seize felt that this was a good lead, even, perhaps, a great lead. He thanked Oscar for his time, and returned to the command center to write in his notebook.

After what seemed like an interminable morning, it was finally time for lunch. Needless to say, everybody on the case opted to eat on the job, scarcely slowing the pace of the investigation as they collected and ate their plates of meatballs, potatoes and lingonberry jam. After lunch, when Edinburgh South Chief Constable Simon Seize thought that Engerlbert's guard would be down, he approached the young co-worker for a chat.

"So Engelbert, what are your feelings about lingonberry juice?"

"I don't know," replied Engelbert. "It's tasty, I suppose." Where was the lad's enthusiasm, wondered Edinburgh South Chief Constable Simon Seize? The passion had drained right out of him, and it was nothing if not suspicious. Finally, Edinburgh South Chief Constable Simon Seize asked Engelbert to account for his whereabouts on the previous night.

"Wha?" Engelbert was shocked. He didn't know if he had ever

felt so hurt, so misunderstood, so angry. In fact, his face would have turned beet red with anger had it not already been beet red with sunburn.

"Let me get to my belongings in my locker and I'll show you." Edinburgh South Chief Constable Simon Seize motioned for a constable to walk with Engelbert to his locker. After a couple of minutes, both returned. Engelbert placed a piece of paper before Edinburgh South Chief Constable Simon Seize. It was a boarding pass showing that Engelbert had flown from Mallorca back to Scotland, arriving so late that he could not possibly have been anywhere near IKEA Edinburgh the previous night. It would have been after hours, the kitchen would have been deserted, and he would not have had sufficient time to assemble a five by five EXPEDIT unit and then open enough bottles of lingonberry juice to fill all twenty-five spaces. Then there was the freezing time. No, it could not have been Engelbert, at least not acting alone.

Edinburgh South Chief Constable Simon Seize did not want to admit that he did not know what to do next. Luckily, Felicia, who had been taken home and had napped all morning, seemed to have shed her trauma like a non-stick KAVALKAD frying pan ($6.99) sheds food. She said she could not stay away. She wanted to help solve the mystery. So she says, thought Edinburgh South Chief Constable Simon Seize, to himself. He wondered if Felicia had come around to throw the team off track. As soon as Felicia arrived at the command center, her mouth fell open.

"Where did you find my copper hair accessory?! I am so relieved. I know it has nothing to do with the investigation, but my aunt made that for me in her jewelry making class, and it means so much to me! I haven't see it for weeks!" Edinburgh South Chief Constable Simon Seize's heart fell hard and fast, making an almost audible thud. All those Volunteer Police Constables, their long grid search, all the forensics, and it all meant nothing. Or did it? Perhaps Felicia came back to spin a story about how her copper jewelry had been missing for weeks. Perhaps she was nervous. Before long, Edinburgh South Chief Constable Simon Seize had pulled an alibi for the previous night out of Felicia, just as he had pulled one out of Engelbert. But unlike Engelbert, Felicia fully understood Edinburgh South Chief Constable Simon Seize's duty to investigate all leads, all angles, all evidence.

The day was ending, the team was spent, and the restaurant was out of cinnamon buns. They would have to continue their investigation in the morning. Just when Edinburgh South Chief Constable Simon Seize was briefing the team on the next day's plan, in walked Anna. After a long afternoon nap, she was feeling a hundred percent, and decided to come in to work to do some tidying up. Seeing all of the police constables at the command center, Anna walked over to find out what they were up to.

"Hello, Edinburgh South Chief Constable Simon Seize. How nice to see you back at IKEA once again. Will you be staying for supper?"

"It's wonderful to see you, Anna, and I have to admit that I have been snacking on cinnamon buns all day long. You see, we have been called in by IKEA security to investigate a very strange occurrence right over there in the IKEA kitchen."

"You don't say!" Anna looked genuinely surprised. Edinburgh South Chief Constable Simon Seize never would have chosen Anna as the guilty party in the lingonberry popsicle caper.

"How strange," Anna continued. "I dreamed last night that somebody in IKEA's kitchen made giant lingonberry popsicles in a fully assembled EXPEDIT shelving unit. I cannot explain it. I have never had such a strange dream in all my life. It seemed so real."

Edinburgh South Chief Constable Simon Seize, and every other team member, stood perfectly still. Was this a confession? Was Anna psychic? Crazy? Both? All of the above? A and C but not B? Despite his love of solving logic problems, Edinburgh South Chief Constable Simon Seize refrained, moving straight to interrogation. He led Anna to a chair, asked her to sit, and told her that it appeared that she was in a lot of trouble. Anna looked perplexed. Could it be that Anna was not aware of the events that had occurred in the walk-in freezer?

The interrogation lasted for several hours. Except during meatball breaks, the team did not let up on Anna. They allowed her to eat a small dish of meatballs, since depriving her entirely could have been construed as cruel and unusual punishment, in other words torture, and Edinburgh South Chief Constable Simon Seize did not want Anna's confession thrown out for having been elicited under duress.

Finally, Anna broke down, gave up, stopped resisting. She said she was resigned to the fact that she had been the one on duty in the kitchen the night before. She had taken her early dinner, leftovers of a cold fish plate- pickled herring and salmon- that she had started to eat at lunch. She remembered taking the fish out of the leftover container she brought from home, putting the fish on the plate, and eating it. Then she remembered eating a slice of almond cake that tasted so much better than she remembered almond cake tasting on any other day. Then, Anna said, she remembered nothing until she woke up this morning not feeling well. Yet, she had seen the whole caper in her dream. Anna, being an honest sort, had to conclude that she had made the giant popsicles. Still, she never admitted to remembering opening all the bottles of lingonberry juice and pouring them into the giant ice cube tray made out of the EXPEDIT shelving unit that she had obviously assembled.

Edinburgh South Chief Constable Simon Seize was, in a sense, at square one. Yes, he had figured out who was responsible for the lingonberry popsicle caper, but he was no closer to why.

Anna was upset, and reasonably so. Edinburgh South Chief Constable Simon Seize felt that he must persist until he helped Anna understand her actions. Yes, it was beyond the scope of his job. Yes, it was late at night. But he knew in his gut that Anna was a good person, and she needed his help. And so, into the late hours of the night, Edinburgh South Chief Constable Simon Seize and Anna thought and thought. When it was nearly 2 AM, Anna was slumped over a chair at the command center.

Just as she was nodding off, in walked Marcus, Anna's nephew.

"Auntie Anna, there you are! I was so worried about you!" Marcus jogged over to his tired aunt. "What are you doing here at two o'clock in the morning?"

"Oh Marcus," replied Anna, "I have done something terrible." She explained everything to her nephew, and as Marcus listened, Edinburgh South Chief Constable Simon Seize noticed that Marcus did not look surprised. He looked *guilty*.

"Marcus," said Edinburgh South Chief Constable Simon Seize slowly, staring into the young man's scared blue eyes, "I think you have something to tell us. In fact, I am sure of it."

Marcus began: "I am so sorry, Auntie Anna. I am so sorry, Chief Constable Seize. I have done something more terrible than the terrible thing you did, Auntie Anna."

Edinburgh South Chief Constable Simon Seize rose to his feet, raised his index finger in the air, and although there were only three of them in the vast dining area, called out to the whole restaurant, "It was the *fish* container, my lad Marcus, wasn't it!"

Marcus could not believe his ears. How did Edinburgh South Chief Constable Simon Seize know? It was beyond plausible that he could have derived the truth from the clues at his disposal. Edinburgh South Chief Constable Simon Seize stared at Marcus, grinning like a maniac.

"Simon! Marcus! What are you two on about? Somebody please explain!"

"Anna, Anna, I can explain everything now," chuckled Edinburgh South Chief Constable Simon Seize, as he sat down at the command center and guiltlessly tossed a few stale cinnamon bun crumbs into his mouth.

"You see, it is all a matter of logic. Our first suspect was Felicia, because we found her hair accessory in the walk-in freezer. Our second suspect was Engelbert because he seemed unnaturally blasé about lingonberry popsicles. And our third suspect was you, Anna, because by your own admission you had dreamed the whole caper."

"What do these three suspects have in common? Dead leads. Evidence that means nothing. Innocence. Let me explain. Felicia's copper hair accessory had nothing whatsoever to do with the lingonberry popsicle caper. Her red hair ring was a red herring. Engelbert's boarding pass from his flight from Mallorca last night appeared to me, half covered by other papers. I spied the word fragments *Herr Eng*. His name appeared this way since he and his family flew Lufthansa. And, Engelbert's German name and his *red* sunburn had nothing to do with the caper. And finally to you, Anna. You had a cold leftover supper of actual red herring and salmon. Your red herring was not an approximation of the term, but actual red herring. Therefore, the logical puzzle tests the principle of bivalence. If false instances of the term "red herring" are false clues, then true instances of the term "red herring" must be real clues. But the truth of a red herring is that it is not a true clue at all. So, we must ask, how can a clue be both true and false? The only way is if the clue is really two clues. And this is what has happened. Anna, I listened to your phone message, the one you left early this morning, explaining why you would were staying at home. I know from constabulary experience that the place young Marcus here had been visiting, the place you mentioned, Anna, the grounds of the Northern County District Lunatic Asylum, are above average terrain for mushroom foraging, especially the, shall we say, very imaginative variety. Anna, you look confused. Let me elaborate. Your nephew collected hallucinogenic mushrooms in your leftovers container, and you mixed your salmon and herring in with them and ate the whole thing! Anna, you have been on a hallucinogenic drug trip!"

"I can't believe it! Marcus would not be involved with drugs!"

"Auntie Anna, Edinburgh South Chief Constable Simon Seize is right. I did not understand what was happening to me. I saw all kinds of flashing lights and dinosaurs in the highlands, and the grass appeared bright pink to me. I said nothing because I did not want to sound like a naïve American. I was burning with curiosity, though. I needed to go back to see if Inverness looked the same when I returned several days later. It did not. The Scottish Highlands are actually quite green, like in all the travel books. I feel terrible. What can I do to make this up to you both?"

Anna smiled warmly. "Oh Marcus, my silly nephew. I will not tell your parents. Nobody got hurt, and I was the subject of a police interrogation, which will only enrich my otherwise bland memoirs. No harm done!"

"You are a good, honest young man," said Edinburgh South Chief Constable Simon Seize. "I am sure that IKEA will be understanding and allow you to repay the cost of the EXPEDIT unit and all the Lingonberry juice by working in the store. As for me, I would welcome you as a guest speaker in our outreach program on the perils of both intentional and inadvertent drug use. Your participation would fit in to Part B."

Anna and Marcus thanked Edinburgh South Chief Constable Simon Seize for his time and effort, and for his mastery of the art of logic. They left arm in arm, already looking back on the episode with humor.

Edinburgh South Chief Constable Simon Seize smiled a broad smile, and sighed. He packed up his briefcase, got into his car, and drove home to resume work on the Saturday crossword puzzle.

FLOW CHART

Drive to IKEA à Cinnamon bun with icing and two cups of coffee, (2-5 PM, $1) -> Sugar/caffeine rush -> Outer space décor theme holds strange appeal -> Purchase 3 FILLSTA orange table lamps on tripods (resemble lunar modules) @ $16.99 each -> Drive home ->Hypoglycemic crash into unconsciousness rationalized as spontaneous "nap" -> Remorse, panic, frantic search for receipt -> Find receipt, relax, plan to return all three lamps -> Still groggy, place three boxed lamps in basement -> Suppressed (in basement) shame -> [Repeat Cycle]

SESTINA

My new room, an empty box
It needed color, shape and light
It also needed art and shades
But that was not all, there was more
I began my strange vague search
Drove straight to my favorite store

IKEA is my favorite store
A jolly blue and yellow box
There's nowhere else I'd take a search
And many ended in its light
A patron could not ask for more
('cept for those recalled blinds and shades)

Oh no! Stunned, I reached for my shades
Who knew *he*'d be in this store!
After years at odds, I'd cried "No more!"
Refused to haggle, bitch or box
Right in this store, had shut the light
Finally stopped our dead-end search

Was this fate? No! His willful search!
I'll hide at once behind the shades
He won't see me in the low light
Why'd he tail me to this store?
I returned his ring, plus the box
What else could he want? What more?

We'd shopped here often, and what's more
We'd sent many friends here to search
Our home had been a trendy box
Our troubles unseen behind bright shades

False poster couple for this store
Truth? CFL blue, our cold light

Lately, my thoughts of him were light
I thought I'd see his face no more
But lo, he finds me in this store
The despised object of his search
I step into view, toss my shades
He lunges, thank God I learned to box

Security is called to the floor of the store, sirens, chaos, a strobe light
Quick, think outside the box! IKEA- a big box, yes! But so much more!
Where we are called to search, for life, for lights, and for my tossed shades.

OBITUARY

EXPEDIT, of Älmhult, Sweden. EXPEDIT, an IKEA shelving unit made of squares in rows or grids, has been discontinued as of April, 2014 after a fatal redesign at IKEA, Sweden. EXPEDIT had been produced and sold for generations and gradually rose to product stardom among its peers both inside and beyond the walls of IKEA stores. EXPEDIT was a versatile shelving unit, available in many sizes ranging from one to twenty-five cubes, two finishes and several colors. Considered essential to those harboring large collections of vinyl LPs, the loss of EXPEDIT has prompted outcry, protest, and a facebook page (mostly "liked" by people in Germany,) dedicated to saving the product. EXPEDIT's demise is a result of its popularity, which led to its scrutiny by global resource stewardship interests. IKEA will replace EXPEDIT with a nearly congruent product called KALLAX. The main difference between the two products is that KALLAX has a slightly thinner border, and so uses somewhat less wood. It has been said that IKEA uses one percent of all wood harvested in the world, and so saving even a small amount of wood on a product that sells millions of units multiplies to substantial forest conservation. The interiors of EXPEDIT and KALLAX are identical, so vinyl collectors may add KALLAX to walls of EXPEDIT without compromise. The consensus among EXPEDIT owners is that EXPEDIT was a loyal and exceptionally patient shelving unit, as well as a good listener. It loved to store books, vinyl records, and baskets of mittens. It loved to divide rooms. "A divided room makes for a united family," EXPEDIT was heard saying more than once. EXPEDIT is survived by hundreds of IKEA storage relatives.

NURSERY RHYME

Old Mother Hubbard
Went to the cupboard
To give the poor dog a bone;
When she came there,
The cupboard was bare,
And so the poor dog had none.

Old Mother Hubbard
Had purchased her cupboard
From an online guy named Ed,
Ed's price was too high
Which left Hubbard dry
And left her poor dog underfed

Old Mother Hubbard
Will buy her next cupboard
From a highly trusted source
She'll design it herself
Not buy off the shelf
That source is IKEA, of course

ICELANDIC SAGA

Gisli, Dyri and the Faraway House.

Chapter 1

It was in the warm days of the midnight sun, in the modern time not long before the tumble of the crowns, that a man brought his ship to Iceland, into Reykjavik the city, from Norway, his name being Gisli. Not on board his ship were his father or mother or sister, who lived ages ago in Iceland but who sailed their ship to Norway when Gisli was a young boy. Gisli was tall two meters and aged eighteen winters, a brooding young man but goodly. In the autumn Gisli moved his house southward down from the heath, and set up a home at a place called Icelandic Academy of the Arts. Gisli dwelt in this land of artists and writers of plays all of thirty-three moons. He was happy enough.

Chapter 2

One night, asleep upon a sheepskin that he coveted for writing musings aplenty, Gisli dreamt that there came a man to him, and said: "There liest thou, Gisli; flit thy house away east across the North Atlantic Ocean for with me all thy good luck awaits thee." Thereupon he awoke and did wonder in what manner he should act. A patient young man with a belief in the strength of goal oriented therapy, Gisli passed eighteen days reading Jungian dream analysis, seeking to interpret his dream and proceed accordingly.

After some time and with no further clarity, Gisli flitted his belongings down to his ship and sailed to London to find the man of his slumbering adventure. Gisli navigated his ship and his future by dreams alone, and found the man from Morpheus, who sat in the manner of waiting. The man had a name which was David. David was as small as Gisli was tall. Gisli and David broke bread, ate fish, and drank ale.

Chapter 3

Gisli and David grew to be friends, making it their wont to waste many afternoons at pub. They drew ugly faces and pretty ideas upon cocktail napkins, using toothpicks dipped in Campari. David was a jocular man with and without ale, and with ale, a man of clever phrases. Gisli and David busied themselves with a story. To no man did they speak of this story until the story was set down on parchment, expressed in the dramatic genre. Gisli and David went half-shares in the play story, traversing the stony countryside with their parchment draped over the back of an old Cleveland Bay. Dramatic readings in public libraries and coffeehouses were their offering, oats and ale their recompense. Word of Gisli and David's drama spread through the English countryside. Not being men of numbers or monies, Gisli and David knew not the ways in which their drama could be contrived to become a blockbuster.

Chapter 4

There was a man named Dyri, born and dwelt both in Reykjavik. Dyri perchance at this time sojourned in England. Dispatched by his medical team to the English lowlands to breathe the floral airs, Dyri passed his days sleeping, and when he could, sitting outdoors on a simple stool, reading poetry and painting landscapes in the tradition of John Constable. Well off for live-stock, Dyri was skilled in numbers and monies, and never suffered hunger or want of anything. Except for his health, Dyri had it made in the shade. He swore to the painterly cumulus clouds above that if ever his health should improve, he would travel to foreign lands to spread mirth and meaning to the corners of the souls of those who also suffered. Chance soon would bring this to pass.

Chapter 5

Dyri did hear Gisli and David's drama read at a nearby pub which Dyri visited daily in order to take medicinal tonics. Gisli and David's drama brought to the stage the story of Gregor, by Franz Kafka, who was not Icelandic but who did enjoy visiting the hot springs from time to time. The drama begins as Gregor, a young man dwelling with his father and mother and sister, does wake at dawn. He is horrified as he does realize that the darkness of night has transformed him into a wretched insect of some kind. Gregor's family discovers Gregor soon thereafter. The drama paints a dystopic picture of Gregor's trying and hopeless life as a bug. Gregor's family reviles him, and he does flinch and cower at every totalitarian blow to the family's tenuous peace. After some time, and by no surprising event, Gregor does cede his life. In his exit, Gregor escapes the familial regime of rage and terror.

Chapter 6

Dyri overheard David and Gisli speak of their vision for the drama. Due to their limited expertise and their small means, David and Gisli expected only to pass their lives as simple laborers, their practice of the dramatic arts never growing beyond a minor avocation. Dyri, suddenly feeling flush in his cheeks, did skip across the room, calling out to David and Gisli. "I have a bargain to make with thee," called Dyri. "Thy business shall be to travel the world with me and read thy drama in houses filled with eager and wise souls. From these persons we shall invite and collect appreciation one from each in the form of a paid ticket." David and Gisli both dumbstruck were. Never had they encountered such a brilliant visionary. Continued Dyri, "Do now as I tell thee, for I am gifted in the ways of theatrical production. Do seek, find, and engage for recompense one actor per written part in thy drama. We shall, all of us, set sail on a circuit of all the great drama houses of the globe, reading your drama over and over."

Chapter 7

Now Gisli did set sail for Norway to say goodbye to his family before sailing the world with his artistic brethren. To all who had known him, there in Norway, Gisli said, "I shall betake myself to Iceland once more, to join a herd of dramatists, to then set sail and to read our drama over and over in all the great drama houses of the globe." To this, Gisli's mother said not one word. She cast a sideways glance at Gisli's father. Gisli's father also said not one word, looking down at his shoes, which were unremarkable. Gisli's younger sister reached for her violin and began to play DUSTY OLD DUST, by Woodie Guthrie, singing, "So long, it's been good to know yuh, so long, it's been good to know yuh, so long, it's been good to know yuh, This dusty old dust is a-blowin' me home, And I got to be driftin' along." Gisli left his family's house and never returned.

Chapter 8

Gisli suffered a minor breakdown, but good fortune was with him as he had privacy and hours to ponder as he sailed back to Icelandic to join the other dramatists. As he knew, he must advise himself toward a merrier disposition. His mother's and father's cold reactions and his heretofore sweet sister's mean-spirited serenade stunned Gisli, not because they were a surprise, but because they were nearly exactly the same as one of the scenes from his and David's play. Gisli realized that like Gregor, he himself was a foreign creature in his family's eyes. He learned then that he had released his subconsciously held beliefs about himself into his drama. Gisli resolved to be free forever, finally happy to have escaped the torture he had endured, raised up in a joyless, closed-minded family.

Chapter 9

Gisli arrived in Reykjavik with renewed vigor and dedication to the arts. There, he and David set about selecting dramatists of the stage to accompany them and Dyri on their journey to drama houses around the world. The dramatists prepared for their odyssey, collecting their chattels on dollies and stowing them on the ship. Days prior to the dramatists' departure on the high seas, Iceland's currency tumbled violently and far, such that all of the banks in the land were forced into receivership, in an effort to avoid the mire of national bankruptcy. Over four winters, Iceland's systemic bank failure taught the dramatists to set their trust in the Icelandic crown no more. A movement was underway, one to avoid a plunge into another strife financial. Advocates of this movement rallied to adopt the Canadian dollar as the official Icelandic currency.

Chapter 10

Dyri, whose wisdom in matters linked to monies was esteemed throughout the land, (and who had been one of the main Icelandic investors in the UK as he could see the crisis coming on,) supported the Icelandic movement to adopt Canada's currency. He created signage to hoist above the demonstrators. He rallied with the other dramatists in the chaotic streets of Reykjavik. He wore a likeness of the Canadian dollar coin, the Loonie, on a giant gold leaf sprayed circular sandwich board. Dyri and others recognized Iceland's and Canada's similarities as northern, resource-based economies, and believed in their hearts that Iceland's sparse population would have little effect on the Loonie's value. Although Dyri and others supported this movement with all their hearts, the currency adoption remained luckless, and the Icelandic crown remained upright.

Chapter 11

Dyri and the dramatists attempt to establish roots in The United States of America, but this effort, like this chapter, filed quickly for Chapter Eleven. Both are now bankrupt.

Chapter 12

For many moons did Dyri and the dramatists reel from the failed currency ties to Canada. They wished to dwell in Canada, longing to bring their play to Canada's northern audiences. With this end in mind, Dyri laid down his sorrows and searched for a sign that would bring him and his friends across the cold Atlantic Ocean. Much joy spread among Dyri's friends when their play was secured for forty nights across the Atlantic, at the Royal Alexandra Theatre. This drama house, located downtown Toronto, was renowned and esteemed. Its interiors were plush with red velvets and golden sculptured walls. Autographed portraits depicting famous dramatists reaching back generations lined the walls. An extended run in the King Street theatre district was sweet consolation for the Icelandic dramatists, still financially on unstable, even molten ground.

Chapter 13

Dyri was of merry disposition. Confident was he that he would discover treasures aplenty in Canada. Dyri set out to secure accommodations for the dramatists for the duration of their sojourn in Toronto. Chief among Dyri's search criteria for a house was size, for many dramatists would voyage together. Being sly and swift in the ways of commerce, Dyri set out on the World Wide Web. He quickly secured a furnished house for the group's visit. This he contrived using a residential real estate short-term rental portal called Airbnb. The house's proprietor was the same as the writer of this saga, and she did offer Dyri a verbal and pictorial description of her property to lease. Dyri and the dramatists set sail for Canada and arrived, each with an extra-large red wheelie suitcase, at the house in Toronto.

Chapter 14

Upon entering the house, Dyri and Gisli and the other dramatists were sublimely at ease, for what did they see, but furnishings
from IKEA in every room. They saw an EKTORP sofa, a POANG
chair, many TARVA beds, duvets and pillows and bed linens and
towels from IKEA. They saw cooking sets and dinnerware, flatware and tea towels, all from IKEA. There were armoires and rugs
and lamps and a teakettle and a coffee pot, all from IKEA. They
all exclaimed to one another: "How glorious! How wonderful!
How we knew that our home in Canada would feel like home.
Transported as though instantly to a place so far from home, yet in
our hearts we knew that Canada would embrace us as a familiar
friend. We will sleep soundly on our IKEA beds, bathe and then
dry ourselves with our IKEA towels, eat from our IKEA plates,
and sit on our IKEA chairs. This is a sign that our journey will be
successful." And this is what came to pass. Dyri and the dramatists readied the theatre, rehearsed the readings, and opened the
doors to the souls of Canadians. And the drama was read over
and over again, and it was a glory to behold. And here the tale of
Dyri and Gisli and the faraway home cometh to a close.

ACRONYM & ANAGRAMS

ACRONYM

Ingvar **K**amprad founded IKEA when he was a boy. He grew up on a farm called **E**lmtaryd near the village of **A**gunnaryd. *IKEA* is an acronym of his initials and the initials of his childhood farm and village.

ANAGRAMS

Ingvar Kamprad. Elmtaryd Agunnaryd:

1. *Vagrant dummy. Dry parking land area.*

2. *Raving mad grey. Damn, a yurt parkland.*
        (Anagram by guest author Bing Leasor)

3. *My aardvark, rampaging redundantly.*
        (Anagram by guest author Large Bison)

STREAM OF CONSCIOUSNESS

Catalog under my arm. The furniture is a pretense. Honesty.
Here for the meatballs. There are ten. It's not wrong, it's part
of the plan. They know. They know. They know how good
they are. They use it. And there are ten on the plate. Rolling
around. Rolling around, slowing down in the gravy. Ten perfect
meatballs. Or fifteen or twenty, but I do not dare. Who dares?
Lingonberry sauce conspires with parsley, alluring, but there
are no health benefits. Brown sauce and mash in a warm slush,
marinating pleasure into guilt. I shade my eyes to allow others
their privacy. Eat three, then potatoes, then four, then potatoes,
then three. Pace the sauce. I hate them. I love them. The fat, the
weight, the mountain of mash, berm of mash, snowdrift of mash,
tracks of mash, residue of mash. There was never anything on
this white plate.

COUPLET

A bite-size ball of beef and pork
Perfection on a dinner fork

RECIPE

Köttbullar (Swedish Meatballs) Riff

Meatballs

½ lb. ground beef
½ lb. ground turkey
1 egg
¼ cup milk
1 small onion, very finely chopped
¼ cup breadcrumbs
1 cup boiled potatoes
2 tablespoons butter
salt
pepper

Cream sauce

½ cup half-and-half
1 cup beef broth
1 tablespoon white flour
1 tablespoon butter
salt
pepper

Directions:

Meatballs: Fry onion until golden in two tablespoons slightly
darkened butter. Mash potatoes. Mix all ingredients well.
Shape into balls. Fry on medium heat in golden butter until
meatballs seared, partially crisped to a nice Jonsboda brown.
Finish in oven until cooked through, about thirty minutes in a
350-degree oven.

Cream Sauce: Melt butter in pan. Add flour. Whisk until Idemo beige in color. If your sauce is Kivik chair beige, you have probably added too much flour. Add beef stock and cream until sauce is Tygelsjö beige. Season with salt and pepper.

Serve meatballs and sauce with boiled potatoes, lingonberry-colored lingonberry jam and single sprig of Tanem green parsley.

HELP WANTED AD

IKEA Group, Älmhult, Sweden, seeks a full-time person to work in our offices. Consistent with IKEA's vision is "to create a better everyday life for the many people," the successful candidate should have considerable experience living a better everyday life. Salary commensurate with experience.

Position involves sitting in a VILGOT swivel chair, on a KOLON floor protector, and, from time to time, in a STOLJAN conference chair in the meeting room. Successful candidate will have use of a BORGSJÖ desk, with the potential to move up to a BORGSJÖ corner desk after one year, and one FORSÅ work lamp, with the potential to move up to a BAROMETER work lamp after one year.

As a full time employee, successful candidate will qualify for one DOKUMENT wastepaper basket, one PLUGGIS recycling bin, one KVISSLE letter tray, and one SUMMERA pull-out keyboard shelf, discounts on meatballs and French fries, and health insurance with a zero deductible on cardiology care.

To apply, write a letter of introduction on a page of a VINTRIG notebook and post to our corporate offices.

LIMERICK

There was a young man from Tobago
Who suffered from painful lumbago
His doctor had said
That a harder new bed
Would be an improvement over the couch in his Winnebago

A past trip to IKEA San Diego
Made him recall mattresses harder than Lego
No need for car or brawn
They'll ship from San Juan
It's the closest store in his archipelago

SOCRATIC DIALOGUE

CRATYLUS

(A Dialogue based on a Dialogue by Plato, Translation by Benjamin Jowett)

PERSONS OF THE DIALOGUE: Socrates, Ingvar, Cratylus.

SETTING: IKEA Athens, restaurant, 10 AM Tuesday, Many Tuesdays ago.

INGVAR: Look, here comes Socrates! Shall we make him a party to the argument?

CRATYLUS: Yes!

INGVAR: Socrates! Socrates! Over here! Please come and join us, and fetch us all another cup of coffee, would you, and perhaps another round of cinnamon buns.

After only a moment, due to the swift service and maximal efficiency in the IKEA restaurant cafeteria-style restaurant, Socrates arrives with morning snacks for the group.

SOCRATES: Good morning, Ingvar. Good morning, Cratylus.

CRATYLUS: And to you.

SOCRATES: These cinnamon buns do smell delicious.

INGVAR: I should explain to you, Socrates, that our friend and esteemed IKEA co-worker Cratylus, who currently works on special projects for us, has been pondering IKEA product names. Cratylus seems to think that all names are natural, as opposed to conventional; that there is a correctness inherent in them, which is the same in any language. He states that if all the world were to call me Ingvar, that would not *necessarily* be my name. Tell me, Socrates, as IKEA's premier Athens consultant, what is your own view of the inherent correctness of names?

SOCRATES: Ingvar, thank you once again for retaining my services. Walking around and around the Acropolis with my students does wear thin more than my sandals, after a while. It is nice to be in an air-conditioned environment with a bottomless cup of coffee and delicious pastry, not to mention the employee discount that you have graciously extended to me. I will gladly assist you and Cratylus in the investigation into the nature of names.

INGVAR: I have pondered this matter and to date am not convinced that there is any principle of correctness in names other than mere convention and habit.

SOCRATES: Well, for instance, suppose I call a bookcase a DALSKÄR, and a faucet a BILLY. Do you think this is right?

INGVAR: Yes, Socrates. You give one name, and I another; and in different cities and countries there are different names for the same things, except of course that at IKEAs worldwide, these names would be standardized, though this would be convention, not the names' inherent correctness.

SOCRATES: But if neither is right nor wrong, and names are not relative to individuals, they must have their own proper and permanent essence: they are not in relation to us, or influenced by us, fluctuating according to our fancy, but they are independent, and maintain to their own essence the relation prescribed by nature.

INGVAR: Socrates. I cannot find fault with your logic. Then again, I am lost, not being schooled in logic as you are.

SOCRATES: Then a bookcase should be called a *bookstorer*, or a *bookdisplayer,* or a *bookdistoreplayer*.

INGVAR: A true solution, though cumbersome.

SOCRATES: The argument implies that names should be given according to a natural process, not by whimsy.

INGVAR: I agree, I think.

SOCRATES: Then, as to names: ought not our product namer know how to put the true natural name of each thing into sounds and syllables, and to make and give all names with a view to the ideal name, if he is to be a namer in any true sense?

INGVAR: I suppose so...

SOCRATES: But who then is to determine whether the proper form is given to the bookcase, whatever sort of wood may be used? The carpenter who makes, or the customer who is to use them?

INGVAR: I should say, he who is to use them, Socrates.

SOCRATES: And who will be best able to direct the namer in his work, and will know whether the work is well done, in this or any other country? Will not the user be the one?

INGVAR: Yes.

SOCRATES: And this director of the namer is he or she who knows how to ask and answer questions?

INGVAR: Yes.

SOCRATES: And him or her who knows how to ask and answer you would call a dialectician?

INGVAR: Yes; that would be his or her job title.

SOCRATES: Then the work of the namer is to give names, and the dialectician must be his or her director if the names are to be rightly given?

INGVAR: Yes, that is true. At least I think so. Maybe.

SOCRATES: Then, Ingvar, I should say that this giving of names neither can be a matter, nor the work of chance persons;

and Cratylus is right in saying that things have names by nature, and that not every man is a creator of names, but he only who looks to the name which each thing by nature has, and is able to express the true forms of things in letters and syllables.

INGVAR: Socrates, you are convincing, but I should be more readily persuaded, if you would show me an example of what you refer to as the natural fitness of names.

SOCRATES: My good Ingvar, we have discovered that names have by nature a truth, and that not every person knows how to give a thing a name. The true way to give a name is to have the assistance of those who know, and you must pay them well both in money and in thanks; these are the Sophists.

INGVAR: I believe you are right, although I do despise engaging consultants.

SOCRATES: My dear Ingvar, I see that you have cleaned your plate of the last crumbs of cinnamon bun, and that your coffee cup is empty. Let me fetch us all another round.

Socrates places Ingvar's, Cratylus' and his own coffee mugs on a tray in the positions that the three men have been seated, in order to remember whose mug belongs to whom, and sets out on the briefest of treks over to the beverage/condiment island. He returns after less than two minutes with three mugs filled with steaming coffee, as well as the appropriate number of sugar packets and a small glass half filled with milk, as IKEA dispenses milk in bulk, not in wasteful tiny paper and plastic containers.

SOCRATES: Now, all the names at issue here are intended to indicate the nature of things.

INGVAR: Of course.

SOCRATES: And here I will ask you a question: Suppose that we had no voice, and wanted to communicate with one another, should we not make signs with the hands and the rest of the body?

INGVAR: There would be no choice, Socrates.

SOCRATES: We should imitate the nature of the thing; the elevation of our hands to heaven would mean lightness or upwardness; heaviness or downwardness would be expressed by letting them drop to the ground.

INGVAR: We would have no choice but to communicate in this way, yes.

SOCRATES: And when we want to express ourselves, either with the voice, or tongue, or mouth, the expression is simply their imitation of that which we want to express.

INGVAR: This makes sense.

SOCRATES: Then a name is a vocal imitation of that which the vocal imitator names or imitates?

INGVAR: I wish that you would tell me, Socrates, what sort of an imitation is a name?

SOCRATES: The art of naming appears to be concerned with music and drawing, since there is an essence of color and sound in anything which may be said to have an essence. And if any one could express the essence of each thing in letters and syllables, would he not express the nature of each thing?

INGVAR: Yes indeed.

SOCRATES: So I should expect. But where does the imitator begin? Imitation of the essence is made by syllables and letters; ought we not, therefore, first to separate the letters, and then of compound sounds, and when they have done so, but not before, of rhythms?

INGVAR: Yes, I suppose that makes sense.

SOCRATES: Must we not begin in the same way with letters; first separating the vowels, and then the consonants, into classes, according to the received distinctions of the learned? And when we have perfected the classification of things, we shall give them names, and see whether, as in the case of letters, there are any classes to which they may be all referred; and hence we shall see their natures, and see, too, whether they have in them classes as there are in the letters; and when we have well considered all this, we shall know how to apply them to what they resemble—whether one letter is used to denote one thing, or whether there is to be an admixture of several of them; and so we shall form syllables, as they are called, and from syllables make nouns and verbs; and thus, at last, from the combinations of nouns and verbs arrive at language, large and fair and whole; and as the painter made a figure, even so shall we make speech by the art of the namer or the rhetorician, or by some other art.

INGVAR: That, Socrates, is logical, though it sounds like an awful lot of work for a home furnishing store to undertake.

SOCRATES: A mighty undertaking, building a language is.

INGVAR: Certainly, Socrates. Cratylus says that there is a fitness of names, but he never explains what is this fitness. And because it is nearly lunchtime, I must resolve this product naming issue at once. Cratylus, I fear that you have become too complacent arguing in abstractions. For this reason, I must reassign you immediately to the Returns and Exchanges Department. I have no doubt, Cratylus, that serving the needs of customers who have changed their minds about their purchases or who have miscalculated furniture sizings, will greatly increase your appreciation of practical matters.

CRATYLUS: Ingvar, I understand your practical needs and your decision. I will report to my new post immediately, after lunch.

SOCRATES: I am full with admiration for you, Ingvar. Pray tell me how you have obtained a clear path to the resolution of the nature of names.

INGVAR: Socrates, I have not obtained a clear path to the resolution of the nature of names, however one of IKEA's common sense values is of course *simplicity*. Therefore, in the name of simplicity, IKEA will name our products by convention, not by true nature. We will have categories of products, each category containing a set of names that will be used for products in that category. Thank you, Socrates, for your assistance in this matter. Please take the afternoon off.

CONVENTION/POLICY

§1 The purpose of IKEA's product name convention is to assist both IKEA co-workers and IKEA customers in identifying IKEA products.

§2 Upholstered furniture, coffee tables, rattan furniture, shall be called Swedish place names.

§3 Dining tables and chairs shall be called Finnish place names.

§4 Beds, wardrobes, hall furniture shall be called with Norwegian place names.

§5 Bookcases shall be called titles of occupations.

§6 Bathroom articles shall be called Scandinavian water body names.

§7 Kitchens and kitchen items shall be called grammatical terms, or names of food items, or functional descriptions of the items.

§8 Office chairs and desks shall be called men's names.

§9 Fabrics and curtains shall be called women's names

§10 Garden furniture shall be called Scandinavian island names.

§11 Lights and shades shall be called names relating to from music, chemistry, meteorology, measures, time, and nautical terms.

§12 Bed linens shall be called names of plants and minerals.

§13 Children›s items shall be called names of mammals, birds, and adjectives.

§14 Curtain accessories shall be called mathematical and geometrical terms.

§15 Wall decorations, pictures, frames and clocks shall be called Swedish place names or Swedish colloquialisms.

§16 Carpets, rugs and doormats shall be called Danish place names.

§17 As in any language, regarding rules of grammar and nomenclature, the exception proves the rule. Thus, some products from each department are named using words falling outside of the categories set forth in § 2 - § 16 of this Convention.

§18 Food sold in the IKEA restaurant, as well as tables, chairs, dishes, cups and flatware on loan to patrons while they consume their food and beverage, shall be called by their generic names in the prevailing language(s) of the country in which each restaurant is located.

TRIOLET

I have misplaced my shopping cart
Within this endless marketplace
I wandered off to look at art
I have misplaced my shopping cart
Frustrated, ate a berry tart
Resumed the search, picked up the pace
I have misplaced my shopping cart
Within this endless marketplace

AUTOBIOGRAPHY

I was born in Montreal in 1965, a place and time without IKEA. Home contained no Swedish furniture (although our kitchen chairs were Danish mid-century modern teak). Through primary and secondary school, and on through college, life was bereft of IKEA, and so only vague, colorless impressions languish in my memory of these early years.

After college, I attended graduate school in Philadelphia, where I rented one unfurnished bedroom in an otherwise furnished house. In need of a large desk for all of my books, papers, and hefty 1980s computer, I bought an inexpensive door to use as a table. My first ever visit to IKEA, then in the Philadelphia suburb of Plymouth Meeting, was for the single purpose of purchasing two table supports of some kind. I purchased two LOFFE (adjustable wooden trestles, $44.) Finally, my life had begun.

Between 1988 and 2014, there were many IKEA trips for me. I would call ten IKEA stores "my" local store. My first sofa was from IKEA Ottawa, a soft foldout wedge in white and blue mattress ticking. I moved to Los Angeles with my IKEA sofa and married a man who enjoyed shopping with me at the IKEA Burbank. He learned all of the IKEA product names and refused to use nouns such as *table* or *shelf*. I hesitate to blame our divorce on our differences over IKEA product nomenclature, but between us, he was certainly always the more proper, I the more common.

After our divorce, I had occasion to visit IKEA once again, this time back in Montreal. I did not need much, but it warmed my heart to know that in my absence, IKEA had opened its doors in my hometown. I visited not infrequently, if only for a plate of meatballs.

Recently, I bought a huge single-family house with plans to divide it up into several apartments. I have been spending time studying IKEA kitchens, since I need to design and purchase four IKEA kitchens. Usually such a "study" session starts with a drive to IKEA, a ten meatball meal and mashed potatoes, and sometimes even a cinnamon bun, and then a couple of hours playing with kitchen components on the IKEA kitchen design computers.

Before I could do the big renovation, I needed various permits from my city. The permit process for such an involved project can be six months to a year, so I planned to rent out the house furnished, until I obtained permits. During a period of two months, I spent over six thousand dollars at IKEA on simple furnishings (nothing built in.) I bought and assembled six beds, three armoires, fifteen lamps, and eight bedside tables. I also bought eight duvet covers, twenty-three towels, thirty-one bed pillows and seven square cushions.

I do not know what I will do after the big renovation. I may have to buy and renovate another house so that I have a reason to keep shopping at IKEA.

RONDEAU CINQUAIN

Announced three hundred times a day
Over IKEA's store PA
All lights are going LED
The newest swell technology
A light bulb that is here to stay

They light up bright with no delay
Their light's directed in a ray
These lights use far less energy

Announced three hundred times a day
Over IKEA's store PA
All lights are going LED

Much lower cost per day you'll pay
A message we can't overplay
Concerned with resource scarcity
Our marketing philosophy
To teach you this sweet roundelay

Announced three hundred times a day
Over IKEA's store PA
All lights are going LED
The newest swell technology
A light bulb that is here to stay

Light Emitting Diode (LED) Rondeau

Robin Segal c. 1350

PLAY

THE FINGER FABLES OF IKEA

DRAMATIS PERSONAE

RAT – a rat finger puppet
RABBIT – a rabbit finger puppet
LION – a lion finger puppet
FROG – a frog finger puppet
SHARK– a shark finger puppet
PANDA – a panda finger puppet that looks like a dog
ELEPHANT – an elephant finger puppet
MOOSE – a moose finger puppet
PARROT – a parrot finger puppet
TURTLE – a turtle finger puppet

SCENE I
On Merchandise Shelf, Children's Section, IKEA Brooklyn, New York, USA. 5 AM.

SCENE II
Upon MAMMUT Children's Table ($39.99), Children's Section, IKEA Brooklyn, New York, USA. Later that day.

SCENE III
Upon MAMMUT Children's Table ($39.99), Children's Section, IKEA Brooklyn, New York, USA. The next day around noon.

THE FINGER FABLES OF IKEA

SCENE I

SCENE. *Upon a merchandise shelf in the Children's Section of IKEA Brooklyn, New York, USA. The time is 5 AM. The store is dimly lit and nine of ten finger puppets are asleep in their packaging.*

RAT: *[Waking Up and Stretching]* Another day in paradise.

RABBIT: Oh! Rat! You startled me! I was asleep!

RAT: *Man up, Rabbit, you quivering puffball.*

LION: Rat, please be quiet. Some of us are still trying to sleep.

FROG: It's no use, Lion. Once Rat is awake, everybody has to be awake.

LION: I know you are right, Frog, but maybe *one* day he will listen.

SHARK: What day *is* it?

RAT: It's Friday. What's it to you, Shark?

SHARK: Only one more day until the weekend! I love the weekend. There are so many children here on the weekend, so much activity. Weekends make me *so* happy!

RAT: Give me a *break*, Shark.

FROG: Really, Rat, do not be so mean to Shark. Let Shark be happy. Let him enjoy his positive perspective on life as a finger puppet. I think you are resentful because people old and young are terrified of real sharks. If we all were the real animal versions of ourselves, he and not you would be the fear monger among us. You know, people do not fear rats as much as they are *disgusted* by them. Also, it is much easier to set a trap for and catch a rat. Sharks must therefore be more intelligent than rats.

LION: Rat *hates* you, Frog. You are exceptionally smart, particularly for an amphibian. This makes Rat even more resentful. Why can't more of us be happy all the time, like Panda?

PANDA: Good morning, everyone! It's going to be a beautiful day! I think I will head down to the marketplace to eat some bamboo.

LION: Panda, please remember that you are a finger puppet. You can't eat.

PANDA: Oh yeah, I always forget that I have no digestive tract.

RAT: I can't believe I was packaged with this group of idiots.

ELEPHANT: Hey good morning everybody, I have a riddle. Ready? What did the snake who swallowed the cow say?

RAT: We give up, Elephant. What did he say?

ELEPHANT: Moooooo-SSSSSSS.

MOOSE: Yes?

[Silence]

RAT: Ha ha ha! HA HA HA! Moose doesn't get the joke. Moose! It's a cow, see: Moooo. And a snake, see: SSSSS. Put them together: Moooo-SSSSS.

MOOSE: Yes? *[More silence.]* You know, my friends, my name is only one syllable long. Moose. It rhymes with deuce, truce, and orange juice, except nothing rhymes with orange, so technically it only rhymes with juice.

Enter from mid-air, stage right, the parrot finger puppet. Parrot flies down onto the shelf, causing it to clang, startling everybody except for the sleeping turtle, whose shell has insulated him from all sounds of the early morning.

PARROT: Listen up, everybody. We have a problem, a BIG problem.

LION: Parrot, where have you been all night?

PARROT: I have spent the night in the office, going over our sales figures.

MOOSE: What do you mean by *sales figures*, Parrot?

PARROT: Oh Moose, we have been over this a hundred times if we have been over it once. We all, the ten of us, are finger puppets. We are a product at IKEA. We come in a cardboard and plastic package and sell as a set of ten for the bargain price of $9.99. OK?

MOOSE: OK.

PARROT: We were designed by Anna Efverlund and our product name is TITTA DJUR, which, roughly, is Swedish for WATCHDOG.

MOOSE: OK, I think I understand.

PARROT: So last night there I was, at the computer, analyzing our sales. I had a small wager going with VANDRING UGGLA.

MOOSE: Who is VANDRING UGGLA?

PARROT: You know, that owl puppet over there. He is so full of himself because he is a *hand* puppet and we are just *finger* puppets. Well, so what, I say, he costs five bucks and is only one character. At a buck a finger, same as us, he should put a lid on his whole superiority head-trip.

MOOSE: What's a head-trip?

PARROT: Never mind that. So anyway, we had a small wager going, over our respective sales. The bad news is that owl's sales are greater than our sales, both at this store and across the United States. I could not access the international data. The worse news is that even owl's sales are pretty stinky.

MOOSE: What's the good news, Parrot?

PARROT: [yelling] There is no good news, you annoying moose.

LION: Parrot, do not yell at Moose. He is trying his best. Now, Parrot, this is indeed disturbing news. Of course we have seen products discontinued due to poor sales. Do you think this could happen to us?

PARROT: It sure could.

SHARK: I don't think we should worry about it. Everything will be fine.

PANDA: Yeah. Let's go to the marketplace to eat some bamboo.

FROG: This is indeed a serious situation. We all, well, except for Shark and Panda, and, um, maybe Moose, need to put our heads together and come up with a plan. Somebody knock on Turtle's shell, wake him up and fill him in. He needs to help out. He might be a slow thinker, but he is practical and his ideas are sensible.

RABBIT: I'm scared! We are going to die! We are going to die!

LION: Hang on there, Rabbit, calm down. We are going to work together to find a way to turn our situation around.

End of SCENE I.

SCENE II.

SCENE. *Upon a pale green MAMMUT Children's Table ($39.99), Children's Section, IKEA Brooklyn, New York, USA. Later the same day.*

LION: Come on everybody, break time is over. We need to make a decision here. Let's review our progress. We have decided, as a group, that since we are puppets, it makes sense for us to perform a puppet show in order to motivate shoppers to buy us. And we all agree that we do not have much time, so we need to be ready to perform by lunchtime tomorrow, when the store is full. So, now, do we have some ideas for a play we can perform? The play cannot be too long or complicated because shoppers do not have long attention spans.

PANDA: We could do a musical number about bamboo! We could sing about its versatility, its use as food, fabric, or strong but light building material.

FROG: Thank you for your input, Panda. There are no bad ideas. There are, however, ideas that might be quite a lot less worse than Panda's. Anybody else have any ideas?

RAT: How about we do a cooking demo in which we roast a rabbit, make frogs legs, and grill some shark! Ha ha ha!

FROG: Now Rat, try to be realistic. And kind. Try to be kind.

TURTLE: I have an idea. Why don't we act out those precious little fables, the ones that usually contain two animals. We are enough animal puppets that we could typecast ourselves. Rabbit and I, of course, could act out The Tortoise and the Hare.

RABBIT: What if I forget my lines? What if we fail? I can't do this!

FROG: Seems to me our physical likenesses do not necessarily match our psychological profiles. Rabbit, unlike the hare in the fable, is insecure and convinced he will fail. The Rabbit in the fable was overconfident. And although Turtle is a good fit for the part of the tortoise, it might throw people off to see a non-rabbit playing the hare, while a turtle plays the tortoise. I believe we should either typecast based on physical characteristics, or hold open auditions.

PARROT: Frog, we do not have time to hold open auditions. Besides, others outside our group of ten might try to audition. The last thing we need is the giant owl hand puppet interfering in our work.

FROG: You are right, Parrot. Good thinking.

PARROT: So what is it going to be?

SHARK: I really want to play the part of the tortoise. I know I am a shark, and I am fast, but emotionally, I understand the importance of constant motion, of never taking breaks, of always thinking about the next step. Please, I know I can do a great job.

LION: Shark makes a good case. Does anybody have a reason to deny SHARK this opportunity?

[There is silence. All the puppets look at each other.]

FROG: Very good, then Shark will play the role of the tortoise.

SHARK: Um, just one little thing. Seeing as that I am, like, a water creature, and everything, I think we need this fable to be set in the ocean. You know, a swimming race, not a land race.

RABBIT: Help! I can't swim! I'm going to drown! Help! Help! Don't let me drown!

FROG: Rabbit, calm down! Do *no*t worry! You do *not* have to play the role of the hare. You do *not* have to swim. It's going to be OK. Just sit down and relax and try not to worry about anything.

[Rabbit hyperventilates, gradually managing to calm himself down.]

LION: Now, who would like to play the overconfident hare?

[Every puppet looks down at the floor, except the frog.]

FROG: Hey, it's called *acting*. If nobody wants to look stupid and lose the race to the shark, I will play the overconfident hare. And since our fable will take place in the water, my being a frog is helpful. And, like the hare, I can be fast because I can hop great distances.

LION: Then it is settled. Our first fable will be The Tortoise and the Hare, performed in water by the Shark and the Frog, respectively.

ELEPHANT: I volunteer to be the director because elephants run in a herd.

RAT: That makes *no* sense at all, Elephant.

ELEPHANT: What I am saying is that I am good at choosing a direction and then going over that way.

LION: Hmm. I see your point, Elephant, but perhaps you could *herd* our audience members over to the stage area, and *direct* them to their seats before the show.

ELEPHANT: I *love* that idea, Lion! Yay! I get to herd persons!

PARROT: I would like to direct this production of The Tortoise and the Hare. In order for the Shark and the Frog to act on a proper wet stage, we will need a shallow pan of water. We need an accomplished set designer and a capable stage manager to select a vessel for the water and figure out how to fill the vessel.

TURTLE: I can figure that out. If I just keep thinking about it, I know I will find the answer.

PARROT: OK, that's good enough for me. Turtle, you've got the job. Now go find a giant pan, and fill it with water right on this MAMMUT Children's Table ($39.99).

TURTLE: I might have a hard time getting up and down from the table.

PARROT: Good point, Turtle. We can borrow a TROGEN footstool ($24.99) and drag it next to the table so that you can make it onto the table in three hops instead of one impossible leap.

FROG: Alright then, our first fable is all planned, except for the technical details, but Turtle is right on top of that challenge. Now, we need a second fable so that the actors in one fable can rest while the other fable is being performed. Does anybody have any ideas for our second fable?

LION: I think it is natural for us to perform the fable of The Lion and the Mouse.

ELEPHANT: I do not know that fable, Lion. How does it go?

LION: Once upon a time, a lion caught a mouse in his paw, and just as he was about to eat the mouse, the mouse said, "Stop! If you do not eat me, one day maybe I will do something nice for you." The lion could not imagine how the mouse could ever help him, but he let the mouse go. Not long after, the lion was caught in a net. The mouse happened to walk by and the lion asked the mouse to chew a hole in the net so that the lion could escape. The mouse chewed the hole, the lion escaped, and the moral of the story is that no act of kindness, however small, is ever wasted.

ELEPHANT: What a great fable!

LION: Since we are taking some artistic liberties with our casting choices in our first fable, perhaps a more traditional interpretation for our second fable would be well received. I would be happy to play the part of the lion.

[Lion, Parrot, Turtle, and Frog say nothing, but stare at the Rat.]

RAT: Why is everybody staring at me? Wait, you think I look like a mouse? A *mouse*? I have never been so insulted in all my life. A **mouse**! Look, there is *no* way I am playing the part of a mouse. I don't care if we as a product get discontinued. I will go it alone. I will figure something out. After all, I am a *rat*. I am clever. I am a survivor.

LION: Alright, it is clear as day that Rat is not going to be much of a team player. What are our other options?

PARROT: Hey, what about that big lug over there, Moose. Moose is only one letter different from mouse. What would be really funny is if we call the fable The Lion and the *Moose* and play it straight, as though it was originally written that way. Moose is so big and goofy, it will be fantastic.

FROG: I think Parrot has a good idea. Since we are all finger puppets, and all basically the same size, people who do not know the fable won't realize that we are playing with body size, and people who get the joke will enjoy it for what it's worth. Moose might not realize why he is getting so many laughs, but what else is new.

LION: Alright then, I think we are in a good position to capture some attention tomorrow, motivate shoppers to buy finger puppets, and stay on IKEA's shelves for a long, long time. Let's do some practice runs and then get a good night's sleep so that we are fresh in the morning. There is a lot at stake for us.

End of SCENE II.

SCENE III.

SCENE. *Upon a pale green MAMMUT Children's Table ($39.99), Children's Section, IKEA Brooklyn, New York, USA. The next day around noon.*

LION: Where are Rabbit and Turtle?! We sent them to the restaurant for audience refreshments over two hours ago. They should have been back by now. Our fables have been rehearsed, our actors are ready, the sets are beautiful, and people are starting to mill around, curious about a bunch of finger puppets frozen in their positions on a pale green MAMMUT Children's Table.

PARROT: Lion, don't worry about Turtle and Rabbit. Now, I don't want to imply that they are expendable, but after Turtle delivered on the water stage, his duties were fulfilled. Maybe he is taking his time. And as for Rabbit, you know everything scares him. He might be hiding under a table, unable to unfreeze himself until tonight after closing.

LION: You are right, Parrot. Still, I can't help being concerned. We are after all a theatre company and must take care of one another.

FROG: While we are on the topic of concern, where are Rat and Panda?

LION: Panda finally convinced Rat to go down to the marketplace to eat some bamboo. I bet Rat will come to his senses momentarily and they will be back soon.

[Just then, Turtle comes running to the group faster than he has ever moved, and Rabbit hops casually beside him.]

TURTLE: You will never guess what just happened!

MOOSE: What? What? What?

TURTLE: Rabbit and I were on our way to pick up some little snacks for our audience, as instructed. Now, true to our species,

Rabbit is quite a bit faster than I, and he pulled ahead of me. Unfortunately, Rabbit is insecure, and although he was way out in front, he felt as though he was lagging behind. Rabbit decided to take one of those IKEA showroom shortcuts, you know how you are following the arrows on the floor, and you are in the living room section, and then you walk through an inconspicuous doorway, and everywhere you look is bathroom hardware! Well, Rabbit did something like that, and he got terribly lost. He must have had a panic attack, because eventually he was exhausted, and passed out, leaning against a big old black PAX armoire.

RABBIT: Yes! A big old PAX armoire, it was! Turtle, Turtle, let me tell the next part!

TURTLE: OK, but waste no time, we have a lot to do!

RABBIT: Yes! Yes! Oh, I am so excited! I can't remember anything! Turtle, you finish the story, I am so delighted, I can't keep my head on straight!

LION: Do tell the rest, Turtle. What on earth happened to the two of you?

TURTLE: Well, my feet were feeling quite dry, seeing as the floor of this store is not exactly muddy like a swamp, so I decided to take a brief detour into the men's room to spend a few minutes in the sink, soaking up some moisture. As I left the men's room, whom should I see but Keith. You know Keith, he is the IKEA co-worker who makes fun of Danielle because she comes to play with us during her breaks, and often uses us to reenact scenes from the soap operas she watches. So anyway, Keith sees me, and he gets interested, because of course I am on a journey far from the other finger puppets. So he follows me, and he records my movement on his mobile phone, which has a video camera feature on it. I was on Rabbit's trail, and when I finally found Rabbit, I called his name, like this, "RABBIT!!!!"

RABBIT: WHAT!

TURTLE: Relax, Rabbit, I am just telling the story of when I found you and woke you up. So then, Rabbit was startled awake and started hopping like a hare, hopping super lightning fast, and Keith caught it all on his phone video cam!

LION: Turtle, I see some humor in this story, and some serendipity, but I fail to make a measured connection between the story, as you have told it, and your current elation. Did something else happen?

TURTLE: Oh yes it did. Keith called the cable news channels and told them that there was a real live Tortoise and Hare race happening spontaneously over here at IKEA Brooklyn. He emailed the clip, and in thirty minutes, there were media teams all over the restaurant, and Rabbit and I were answering questions left and right. The video clip has gone viral already. I think we are at a quarter million views, and the clip only hit the net two hours ago.

RABBIT: The IKEA Brooklyn Children's Section Manager has booked a media tour for us. We are all going! We have to pack and be ready to drive to LaGuardia in thirty minutes. First stop, CNN. Second Stop, Animal Planet. We are going to do big group interviews! They promised us a semi-circle of ten tiny bucket seats on an itty bitty stage with little microphones pinned to our chests!

TURTLE: It's all true. Nobody ever expected finger puppets to act on our own, let alone inadvertently enact a famous fable right here in the IKEA showroom.

PARROT: This is major major, boys. And do you know what the bottom line is? The bottom, *bottom* line is that we, *we*, the set of ten finger puppets, are going to sell sell sell like never ever *ever* before.

MOOSE: Parrot, why do you keep repeating words?

PARROT: Don't worry about a thing, Moose. As long as we stay together, everything will be fine from now on.

End.

FABLE

A rabbit finger puppet and a turtle finger puppet departed the IKEA Children's Section and were on their way to the IKEA restaurant for some snacks. True to form, the turtle puppet moved more slowly and the rabbit puppet faster. The rabbit puppet found that the turtle puppet was nowhere to be found, so he doubled back and showed the turtle puppet a shortcut, so that the two could both get snacks at the restaurant in a timely manner.

An IKEA coworker witnessed the rabbit puppet hop once again towards the restaurant, and apprehended the rabbit puppet in a net he kept near his work station. Assuming, based on the famous fable of the tortoise and the hare, that the rabbit puppet was trying to beat the turtle puppet to some prize destination, the IKEA co-worker asked his colleagues what they thought he should do with the tricky, greedy, rabbit puppet.

"Let us make rabbit puppet stew with this tricky, greedy rabbit puppet," said one IKEA co-worker. That was enough to make the rabbit puppet speak up to save his life.

"I was not trying to beat the turtle puppet at a race," explained the rabbit puppet. We had set out together and I helped him out by showing him a shortcut. We were on an errand to bring snacks back to our friends."

The IKEA co-workers were torn. On the one hand, the fable of the tortoise and the hare held a lot of weight, but on the other hand, a talking rabbit puppet with a quick explanation was quite convincing as well. Seeing that he needed to continue persuading the IKEA co-workers, the rabbit puppet told them this fable:

"A Wolf coming out of a field of oats met a Horse and thus addressed him: "I would advise you to go into that field. It is full of fine oats, which I have left untouched for you, as you are a friend whom I would love to hear enjoying good eating." The Horse replied, "If oats had been the food of wolves, you would never have indulged your ears at the cost of your belly."

The IKEA co-workers were stunned to silence, not least because of the rabbit puppet's eloquence. Rabbit continued, "The moral of the story, of course, is that men of evil reputation, when they perform a good deed, fail to get credit for it."

The IKEA co-workers unanimously voted to let the rabbit puppet and the turtle puppet enjoy their honestly acquired treats back on their merchandise shelf.

And the moral of *this* story is that at IKEA, anything is possible.

ODE

... ON A SWEDISH VACUUM FLASK

Thou mass produced, thou simple stainless steel
Thou ever silent upright opaque pot
That holds some heated drink or soupy meal
Whose vacuum seal forever keeps it hot
Thy unadorned exterior pale blue
Speaks of thy confidence, no scribbles there
Nor frivolous designs upon thy cap
Form is a slave to function, this is true
Thy vacuum seal compresses heated air
I keep thee, without burning, on my lap

However strong and independent thee
And though 'bout others often thou trash talks
Just next to thee, we often chance to see
A simple plastic matching sandwich box
Nor did thee shun another witnessed friend
A larger box, perhaps for bread and cheese
So many foods are possible to pack
Placed side by side, or stacked, or end to end
In KULLAR vessels, foods that heat or freeze
All nestled in a bright red cooler sack

COMPARISON

Category	FIFTY SHADES OF IKEA	FIFTY SHADES OF GREY
Title Character	INGVAR KAMPRAD (the IK in IKEA)	CHRISTIAN GREY
Business	Founder and owner of IKEA furniture stores	Communications technology, sustainable energy, shipping, commodities network… basically every business. Except furniture.
Date of Birth	March 30, 1926	June 18, 1983
Business Philosophy	"To create a better everyday life for the many people."	"I don't have a philosophy as such. Maybe a guiding principle – Carnegie's: 'A man who acquires the ability to take full possession of his own mind may take possession of anything else to which he is justly entitled.' I'm very singular, driven. I like control – of myself and those around me."
Number of Employees	150,000	Over 40,000

Lives in	Switzerland/Sweden	Seattle
Vehicle	Used Volvo	Personal helicopter
Net Worth	$4.2 billion (real dollars,) although this is recently down from over $30 billion, (when he appeared in the Forbes top ten *real* billionaires,) after Kamprad transferred most of his wealth to a charity beyond his or his family's control.	$2.5 billion (fictional dollars) (placing him, on the Forbes Fictional 15 of 2013, immediately below Richie Rich, of the comic books, and above Tywin Lannister of *Game of Thrones*.)
Leads by:	Example: Shopping for Christmas wrapping on sale immediately after Christmas, dropping in to IKEA for an inexpensive meal, and writing on both sides of paper.	Control: Once he ties up his "partners," he gets to lead by default.
How his business empowers women:	Provides them with appealing and affordable home furnishings that they can assemble themselves, thereby saving money.	In addition to everything else under his control, his businesses invest "in humanity," whatever *that* means.

FAN FICTION (ETHAN FROME)

Frome stamped on the worn oil-cloth to shake the snow from his boots, and set down his lantern on a kitchen chair which was the only piece of furniture in the hall. Then he opened the door.

"Come in," he said, and as he spoke the droning voice grew still. It was that night that I found the clue to Ethan Frome.

Ethan, still a prisoner for life, had lost his one ray of light. It had been extinguished after all. Mattie sat in a dark corner of the kitchen, no longer vibrant, no longer a ray, no longer lit at all. No longer did the lamplight fall on Mattie's hands. No longer did Ethan wish to remember the night it had. On this night, and on all nights, Zeena and Mattie, flush and tight-jawed, glared at one another, surrounded by mountains of color swatches and bolts of fabric.

Zeena had never had kidney troubles to begin with. She had been concealing her professional decorating education classes, which she took mostly over the internet but which required semi-annual seminars in Bettsbridge. Eventually, she was found out. It could be imagined that Ethan found the laptop, which was kept in plain view by the bedroom wash basin, or more likely the premature presence of electricity in his home, but neither of these anomalies struck Ethan Frome as strange. Since Zeena could not break away to attend commencement at the conclusion of her course of studies, her diploma was sent to her in the mail. Ethan opened it. From that day forward, Zeena spent the destitute family's every spare cent on high-end custom lighting and window treatments. She argued that these elements would make their poor home appear luxurious, as seen from the outside, which is where everybody they knew stayed, unwilling to enter this strange group's home.

Mattie and Ethan took part-time jobs at the Bettsbridge IKEA, which afforded them employee discounts on home furnishings, which they used for anything but lighting and window treatment purchases; on frozen Swedish delicacies (which they indulged in only at the holidays,); and on soft serve frozen yogurt. It was this cold white treat, reminiscent of their tragic snow date, that bound this couple for all eternity, but only during lunch breaks.

VILLANELLE

My kitchen has no ambient light
Why did I paint the walls so dark
Food stains are visible on white

The opposite of dim is bright
A turquoise blob, an orange spark
My kitchen has no ambient light

My lamp shades are a sorry sight
As brown and washed out as a lark
Food stains are visible on white

To you this seems a trivial plight
My furnishings in colors stark
My kitchen has no ambient light

I'll toss a stick of dynamite
I'm sorry for this crude remark
Food stains are visible on white

My nerves are raw, my budget's tight
The light department beckons, hark
My kitchen has no ambient light
Food stains are visible on white

EPISTLE

My dear and ever helpful IKEA store employees, I hope you are
well today.
I write to you as a group today to urge you to do something
about something.
(The first something is up to you.)
(The second something is not your fault.)
You may not know, but nobody looks good in yellow. No, wait.
The only people who look good in yellow also look good in
anything.
They look good draped in a red check plastic tablecloth soiled
with barbecue sauce.
We can eliminate them from our concern.
It is best not to think of them anyway.

The Swedish flag's blue and yellow colors have been adopted by
IKEA.
Although we know this, and although it makes sense in our
minds, wearing yellow for this reason alone simply is not right.

There are very few reasons anybody wears yellow:

First Reason: Yellow is High Visibility.
Bright yellow rubber coated rainwear is a sound idea.
For people sailing freezing cold open waters.
Customer service rarely plays a part in that sector.

Second Reason: Yellow is On Sale.
Garments of yellow are often the last and slowest to sell.
Human beings are bargain hunters and remainder pile foragers.
We love the kill, even though the prey, just by being yellow, is
easy.

Third Reason: Yellow is a Gift.
This is related to the *on sale* reason.
More human nature.
Gift purchases from the sale table.

Fourth Reason: The Optical Illusion of Yellow.
Some believe yellow makes them look tan, therefore more attractive.
And that darker colors do the opposite.
Perhaps yellow really does make one look more tan, but there are alternative strategies.
Wear pink or light blue or white or pale green or lilac or peach.
Or anything but yellow.

Fifth Reason: Yellow Uniform.
Yellow as corporate color plus corporate uniform equals yellow uniform.

Sadly, IKEA has seen fit to dress all of you in yellow.
Not any yellow, though.
The yellow you wear looks like a dirty yellow, like a yellow that used to be bright.
It looks like it once was a sunny yellow.
It looks like a yellow that got thrown in the wash with a brand new black tee shirt.
I have been watching you, all of you, even the happiest among you, the most upbeat. You, helpful, optimistic IKEA employees, every one of you has a sadness about you.
Your dark yellow shirts are a depressed aura floating around you.
Your yellow feels blue.
Speak up. (Do not be yellow.) Ask for change.
Do not be blue. Wear blue!

Ever your most loyal patron,

Robin

TERZA RIMA

In Terza Rima, this poetic form
Italian words are easier to rhyme
In English, it's too tough to be the norm

But Dante, in this form, back in his time
Put forth his classic Comedy Divine
In English, though, it's prose! Poetic crime!

"Without the meter, this thing isn't mine!
Like Billy shelves without the smooth veneer,"
Said Dante, pouring one more glass of wine

And once more Billy's product of the year
To measure up to Billy, this is clear
Is simply to achieve the perfect state

Like classics, Billys don't depreciate

DIARY ENTRY

Dear Diary,

I'm depressed. I know I shouldn't be, but it's just the way I feel and I can't help it. Piling guilt on top of depression doesn't do me any good either. Things used to be different. When I was a kid, I felt like part of a team. We were all young and ambitious. Nobody knew who was gonna make it big, who would be a one season wonder and then be discontinued, and who would be recalled or redesigned, renamed and never mentioned again. Each of us wanted to succeed, of course, but we all cheered for each other as well.

I remember my first model apartment. It was in a store in Dusseldorf, in 1985. I was holding a radio, books, and some framed pictures. I was rarely noticed, being just a black shelving unit, but I was comfortable. Being "part of the furniture" never bothered me. I was proud to blend in during browsing, to be just another off the shelf item. But when it came time to shop for an apartment's furnishings I was rarely left off the list. I had it all: low price, easy assembly, neutral color, reasonable payload. My older cousin William featured molding, expensive hardware and a polymer finish. But he never left the drawing board. It was all Billy, all the time.

My sales shot up. They called me a cash cow. I became a symbol, a mascot. It went to my head and I became aloof from the other products. They called me shelf-indulgent, and I guess it was true, but despite all the glory, all I felt was lonely. The other products that had been with me back in the old days started to die off. I couldn't relate to up and coming stars like EXPEDIT, with their hipster market. I felt ashamed that I was too shallow to hold vinyl LPs. For the first time, I felt insecure and jealous.

Recently I heard that EXPEDIT was being discontinued, redesigned to conserve wood. I didn't think I'd outlive EXPEDIT, of all my shelving cousins, but there it goes into the annals of IKEA product history. And here I am, still kicking. I feel guilty for ever having felt threatened by EXPEDIT or by any other product.

As successful as I seem, I know deep down that I am also ordinary. The love affair with Billy doesn't last. Either people forget about me and take me for granted, crush me with decades of National Geographics, knickknacks and dust, or they dispose of me. Whenever I look myself up on Craigslist, there I am in dozens and dozens of listings. Well, I guess I should be thankful that I am robust enough for there to be a healthy market in pre-owned Billy.

They say I am a top shelf product, but you know, Diary, I also have a bottom.

SPORTS COMMENTARY

(Television Broadcast)

TIM: Welcome back. If you're just joining us, we are *live* at the Sixteenth Annual IKEA Games here in Toronto, Canada. I'm Tim McEh, here with Leif Mapleson, on Canada's Shopping Channel, as well as on multiple cable and satellite feeds worldwide. This first *ever* Shopping Channel Sports Special brings together IKEA shoppers from over *thirty* countries.

LEIF: That's an amazing achievement right there, Tim, but on this final and eighth day of these IKEA Games, this is the day we get to watch what I like to call the *four by four hundred relay* of shopping events. Today, we are seeing the most skilled teams of shoppers perform breathtaking feats of inventory pulling, self-scanning, wheeling carts, and packing merchandise into their vehicles, in an incredible event called the Two Hundred and Fifty Kilogram Full Shopping Experience.

TIM: That's right, Leif. In the Two Hundred and Fifty Kilogram Full Shopping Experience, teams of four, and note that all team members *must* reside in the same household, pull merchandise from the warehouse shelves, self-scan the items, wheel the cart to the loading zone, and load all two hundred and fifty kilograms of merchandise into their *actual* family car.

LEIF: Tim, as a note to our international audience, two hundred and fifty kilograms is about five hundred and fifty pounds.

TIM: Thanks, Leif. The rules of this event state that a maximum of *two* team members may participate in each task. We should clarify that wheeling the cart from checkout to loading zone, and backing the family car up to the loading zone comprise one *single* leg of the relay. The third and fourth family members may *not* direct the driver of the car. We *have* seen some disqualifications as a result of some offside family members screaming at drivers headed for concrete pillars and barriers. Such a shame. But that's part of the competition!

LEIF: Tim, thanks for that rundown of the event. So far this afternoon, we have seen teams from all over the world compete. In just a minute, we will see the top seeded teams from the metropolitan regions of Los Angeles, Stockholm, and seeded third, from right here, Toronto, Canada.

TIM: Leif, a Canadian team has never been seeded higher than fourteenth, but since the Games are right here in Toronto, the Canadian teams have been training like mad. You cannot drive by a closed IKEA without seeing families driving around the parking lot, backing into in the loading area, moving practice merchandise in and out of their vehicles.

LEIF: And here we go! This relay event, already underway indoors, is about to emerge into the outdoors. We are positioned outdoors, with a view of the parking lot and the loading area. Here come the shopping carts! We are looking at the third leg of the four leg relay right now.

TIM: *Wow.* I have never seen so much merchandise piled into one shopping cart. Well, I take that back. I've seen it at the *last* IKEA Games! These teams are impressive! Look how the Swedes have used the height of each item to conserve precious space inside the cart. The Americans are using the sprawled packing method, meaning flat and large on the bottom, with very little height. In this configuration, the center of gravity stays low. All I can say about their method is thank heavens for those extra wide automatic double doors! The Canadian team seems to be employing a hybrid carting strategy, borrowing partly from the Americans and partly from the European technique. Typically Canadian, eh Leif!

LEIF: You can say *that* again, Tim.

TIM: The Canadian team seems to be winning the cart race to the loading area, with the Swedes not far behind. The Americans are at a disadvantage with such a large merchandise footprint. They are having trouble getting through the doors. It might not have been wise to place the longest item oriented exactly left to right across the top of the cart. Leif, what can you tell us about the three vehicles heading over to the loading area.

LEIF: Well, Tim, *this* is a bit of a surprise. It seems that the American team from Los Angeles did not equip their vehicle with snow tires, and now they are spinning their wheels in a snow bank in Parking Area F3.

TIM: And remember the rules, no participation by more than two family members in any one leg of the relay.

LEIF: Look, look, the American cart pusher is leaving his wide load between the two sets of sliding doors to run into the parking lot, over to his team car, I'm guessing to push the car out of the snow bank. Ladies and gentlemen, what we are witnessing here is classic American poor planning with an ingenious American creative response!

TIM: The dramatic stumble, crumble and comeback tale is not in the cards this time, Leif. Look, unless the American team has super powers when it comes to packing merch into their car, they are going to have to reckon with the high probability of third place.

LEIF: Isn't that the truth.

TIM: Leif, just look at the Swedes and the Canadians move smoothly from cart pushing to merch loading. The Swedish team driver is the grandmother of the ten-year-old boy pushing the cart. The boy's parents round out the team. Driver has the car right up at the loading dock and the boy has pushed the cart with considerable grace considering that the merchandise outweighs him by a factor of eight. And now, the boy's mother and father take over for the last leg of the relay. Just look at their technique. Father does the lifting, and mother steers placement of the merchandise from inside the cargo space.

LEIF: The American team has pushed their car out of the snow and the cart pusher is now back at the loading zone. They are just so far behind the others in this heat.

TIM: Leif, let's run down the items in the cart.

LEIF: Sure, Tim. Each team in the relay must pull, scan, push and load the following items: one ANEBODA armoire (39 kilograms); two SULTAN FIDJETUN mattresses, queen size (14.9 kilos each); one EXPEDIT five by five shelving unit (94.2 kilos); two BILLY bookcases (37.5 kilos each); twelve GOSA SYREN side sleeper pillows (0.8 kilos each); one six pack of SVALKA red wine glasses (0.9 kilos); and one four pack of VAKEN water glasses (0.9 kilos).

TIM: Thanks, Leif. *There* is something mighty curious: The Canadian team has stopped moving altogether.

LEIF: It's true, Tim. Look at that. *What* is happening?

TIM: The team members are staring at one another, and it looks like they are each *nonchalantly* trying to push one of the BILLY bookcases in opposite directions.

LEIF: Huh? Tim, what am I missing here?

TIM: It sure looks like the Canadian team has fallen prey to a classic family shopping weakness: they are fighting passive aggressively. Of course, everything that one of them does now, the other will sabotage. Once a team spirals down into this pattern, it is pretty much all over. It's too bad, too, since the Canadian team had really improved their basic scanning and loading skills since the last games.

LEIF: Well, Tim, it looks like the Swedes are going to take first place again.

TIM: Yes indeed, Leif, another top prize for the Swedes. But unlike in years past when the Swedes were the clear winners as early in the relay as self-scanning, this one was not decided until the last leg. It is universally true, actually, that since the games have attracted competitive shoppers from outside of Scandinavia, the techniques at these events have developed remarkably quickly.

LEIF: Tim, what do you think is the reason for such developments?

TIM: Well, Leif, self-scanning technology is everywhere now, so one big reason for the overall improvement in this event is as simple as *practice practice practice*. Who among us is not now agile with a scanning gun! I don't know a single person who can't juggle a six-pack of toilet paper in one hand until the barcode faces up.

LEIF: Great point, Tim. Do you think car design has anything to do with the amazing reduction in times we are seeing in the Merchandise Packing segment?

TIM: Could be, Leif. But you have to remember that in this relay event, the smartest competitive shoppers prepack their merchandise into efficient units when they are scanning them and placing them into their carts. This makes it much easier to achieve low times in the Merch Packing segment.

LEIF: Wow, Tim. Sounds like *you* have completed one or two IKEA Shopping Relays yourself!

TIM: Who hasn't, Leif!

LEIF: With IKEA becoming so mainstream, how long do you think it will be before these games will go knocking at the door of the International Olympic Committee?

TIM: Well, Leif, funny you should mention that. IKEA has been talking to the IOC for some time now. It appears that the first event they would like to introduce as a demonstration sport during the 2020 Olympics is Merchandise Packing.

LEIF: No kidding, I would have thought shopping cart wheeling would have been first up.

TIM: It's true, Leif, cart wheeling is indeed practiced by people in more countries, but the IOC has other concerns. Merch Packing is a wonderful sport that requires more than the pushing and running of Cart Wheeling. It combines the skills of weight-lifting and wrestling, which could attract athletes to cross over, or to branch out; the way track and field sees athletes compete in several events at the same Games.

LEIF: You know, Tim, I have heard it said that during the snowy and icy winter of 2013-14, many North American IKEA stores witnessed Merch Packing competitors developing their ice dancing skills as well.

TIM: Absolutely, Leif. And you know something else, the Winter Olympics require that its sports be practiced in at least twenty-five countries over at least three continents, so IKEA Merch Packing would qualify as a Winter Olympic Sport.

LEIF: Let's see, Tim. I get that there are icy conditions in Europe and North America, but on which other continents are there IKEA stores where temperatures fall below freezing and ice accumulates? Doesn't the western part of Russia count as part of Europe?

TIM: Oh my goodness, Leif, IKEA Shenyang is C-O-L-D *cold*! I was up there in China once for an Asian regional Unpack-the-Flatpack competition. Couldn't eat enough meatballs! They were only thing that kept me from turning to a block of *ice.*

LEIF: It looks like the Swedes are finishing up, Tim.

TIM: No surprise there, Leif. Stay tuned everybody. When we come back from break, we'll have all the stats, as well as the medals ceremony.

(Cut to commercial)

OCTAVE

IKEA's been around for many years
The nineteen fifties saw a chair called RUT
The purpose was for "knitting"(!) on your butt
Or listening to birdsong with your ears

Fast-forward over sixty-seven years
Producing pieces, e'er no global glut
Still, just two grand to furnish my whole hut
IKEA, still the master of veneers

SHOPPING LIST

- Fryken
- Öresund
- Ringskar
- Ljusa
- Vesterbro
- Smycka (12) & Socker
- Samspelt
- Mula abacus
- Stopp
- Fryebo
- Bevara
- Potatischips Saltade
- Pepparkaka
- Sylt Lingon
- Köttbullar

Baskets
Toilet seat
Faucet
Flashlight
Rug
Artificial flowers (12) & milk can
Bright green angular deer figurine
Abacus
Anti-slip pad
Battery lamp
Sealing clips
Potato chips
Ginger thins in tin
Lingonberry preserves
Meatballs

PHILOSOPHY

IKEA's philosophy is described by Ingvar Kamprad as a corporate vision: "To create a better everyday life for the many people." This vision, explains Kamprad, is implemented in IKEA's business sector according to something he calls the "bridge technique." The "bridge" begins at one end in the people's homes. IKEA does not design products in the abstract. Instead, IKEA learns people's needs and wishes, including functional, aesthetic, and cost related. At the other end of the bridge are IKEA's production and material requirements. The bridge itself is a middle ground. IKEA does not only "display" its furniture in the showroom, it creates dozens of "home" environments that people can sit in and *feel* at home, right in the store.

Over the decades, IKEA has become successful enough to transfer about ninety percent of its privately held wealth to a charitable foundation. The IKEA Foundation creates a better everyday life for the many *more* people than those who shop at its stores. Among the foundations partners are unicef, Save the Children, The Earth Institute at Columbia University, Refugees United, Clinton Health Access Initiative, Asian University for Women, Water.org, Girls Not Brides, Global Child Forum, Medecins Sans Frontieres.

NARRATIVE NON-FICTION

I was young, not even a teenager, the first time I heard the word IKEA. It was spoken as though French, I thought, pronounced "Ee-kay-ah." There was an accent resembling a forward slash over the E. I did not know it was a Swedish company. I don't think anybody suspected it was an acronym. All I knew is that it was a store, somewhere, a store that sold possibly the ugliest lamp I had ever seen, a lamp with an umbrella shade sitting on what looked like a cheap music stand tripod base.

The person who introduced me to the world of IKEA was my best friend's mother, Joan. She liked her umbrella lamp, but she *loved* the store it came from, and Joan was not much of a shopper, in general. She was more of an innovator, like IKEA itself, searching for better ways to get things done. When I was only five, I discovered her in her living room, standing on her head, red-faced, claiming to be relaxing. She called this strange pastime *yoga*. She was the first person I knew to eat *yogurt*. Ate the age of five, I confused *yoga* and *yogurt* because Joan was the only person I knew who, in 1970, had anything to do with either.

Joan was also the first person I knew who bought a crock-pot. The crock-pot made it possible for Joan to cook dinner while at work all day. After her divorce, Joan raised three kids as she put herself through school, earned a Ph.D. and became extremely successful in her field. So for me, if Joan said IKEA was a fine store, an interesting concept, something to look into some more, I paid attention, despite the ugliness of the umbrella lamp.

HAIKU

Paper floats skyward
Lamp pieces piled high, in trash
Missing instructions

TANKA

Birch veneer stepstool
BEKVÄM, $16.99
There must be a catch
Some assembly is required
You can always return it

WARNING LABEL

IKEA ≈≈SØMÅÏTÂ≈≈ mattress

May slow heart rate.
May cause drowsiness.
May interfere with hyposomnia, insomnia, insomnolence and cacosomnia.
Safety goggles not recommended.
Do not dry clean.
Not dishwasher safe.
Beware the ides of March.
Fatal if swallowed.

ASSEMBLY INSTRUCTIONS

Note: I have assembled six TARVA beds (four double and two queen) using only pictorial assembly instructions. At first I thought these instructions were complicated, but then I realized that *the bed itself* is quite complicated, assembled from a total of 159 pieces of wood, metal and plastic, using two hex keys, two screwdrivers and a hammer. Yet, IKEA has provided me with complete, clear assembly instructions in only nineteen line drawings, plus a handful of clarifying drawings, such as advising us to take this project on with a friend, or enlargements of some of the drawings' details. And this, by the way, no matter which language I speak, and no matter whether or not I am even literate in a single language. I decided to contrast this easy to read instruction manual with a written manual. I have written this manual myself, or, performed a "pictorial to written" translation. So, here they are, assembly instructions for the TARVA bed, written out in English, with no illustrations:

1. To assemble this bed, you will need to supply one Phillips head screwdriver, one flat head screwdriver, and one hammer.

2. If you assemble this bed by yourself, you will be sad. If you assembled this bed with a friend who has a pencil behind his ear, indicating know-how and experience, you will be happy.

3. If you are confused, do not despair. Instead, call IKEA.

4. Hardware included with the boards: a. 8 metal cylinders; b. 43 wooden pegs; c. one long bolt; d. one thing that sort of looks like a screw, but has four sections, the top one being a fitting for a Phillips head screwdriver, the bottom one looking like screw threads but without a pointy tip; e. 8 plastic caps that are threaded inside; f. 12 tiny screws; g. 8 small bolts that are thicker than

the tiny ones; g. one long nut; h. 20 small screws; i. 14 very long bolts; j. one nut that will twist and that has a fitting for a Phillips head screwdriver; k. 14 nuts that bolts fit into in a hole going sideways into the nut, rather than a regular donut shaped nut, and these nuts also have fittings for flathead screwdriver at one end; l. 2 flat metal plates each with several holes in them; m. 2 rails that are roughly the length of the bed; n. 4 metal expandable arms with holes in them, smaller and lighter than the two rails; o. 2 hex keys, of different sizes; p. one mid-beam; q. one appropriately sized unit of wood slats.

5. From among the unidentified pieces of wood, find the one that is square in diameter and that has two different size holes exactly in the middle on the same side, as well as holes close to either end on that same side. In the smaller of the two holes, place the thing described as hardware d. Tighten with Phillips head screwdriver.

6. In the larger hole just beside, insert a wooden peg.

7. Find a small piece of wood that has lots of holes in it, in pairs, on opposite sides. This piece of wood will have a large type of notch in one end. Find another piece of wood the same length as in instruction 5, this time a flat broader one with three holes in each end.

8. Take the other end and with it hole side up at the notchless end, insert the two pegs from 5. And 6. into the two holes. If they fit, remove the pegs (and the attached board) and place hardware piece j. into the hole on the small piece of wood so that the four part hardware piece that you screwed in will fit into it, and when you have done this, use a flat head screwdriver to tighten hardware piece j.

9. The other long piece of wood you found has three holes in each end, and holes on one side. Put those holes facing down. This piece of wood slides into the notch in the smaller piece of wood. Now you should have the first long piece forming a T with the smaller notched piece, and when you add the third piece, you will get an H shape with the notched piece being the

cross bar of the H. The holes at the ends of the second long piece should be on the opposite face from the twisty nut hardware lettered j.

10. You will have a series of holes that meet up in the two parts on either side of the notch, and the board that fits into the notch. From below, place the single long bolt c. and from above, place the long nut g. They have to screw together, but in order to do this, you need to place one hex key in each, and line them up perfectly… Tighten.

11. With the assembled pieces flat on the floor, place wooden pegs (hardware b.) in each of the 16 holes in the notched crossbar of your H made of the three pieces of wood. Onto each set of two pegs, fit one of the eight small slats with pairs of holes on each end.

12. Place wooden pegs into the ends of the longer pieces of wood. On the piece with two holes, put the wooden peg in the larger hole at both ends, and on the piece with three holes, put the wooden pegs in the two outside holes but not the center one. This step requires a total of six wooden pegs.

13. It's time to take two more pieces of wood from the pile. You will need two pieces that are square in diameter, to form the vertical ends of the headboard. These two pieces each must fit onto the eleven wooden pegs protruding from each side of the already assembled portion of the bed.

14. Be sure to place these two new pieces with the holes closer to the floor, as all pieces are still flat on the floor. Slide the new pieces so that the wooden pegs enter their holes.

15. Take the whole assembled unit and turn it over, meaning flip it onto its back. Now the front of the headboard is facing up.

16. You will find two holes on the side edges of each headboard edge piece. Place a long bolt (hardware i.) into each of these holes, but not all the way. Find where the end of the bolt will go, and then find a hole near that place. The hole will be in another

piece of wood.

17. Into each hole, place nuts (hardware k.) turned so that the opening in the side is lined up with the bolt that you have not fully inserted into its hole. Place a flat head screwdriver in the nut to hold it in place, and use whichever hex key fits to tighten the bolt into the nut. Do this for both bolts. Then repeat for the other side of the headboard (2 more bolts). You have completed the headboard.

18. Take the long board that is different from the other remaining long boards, and the two square diameter pieces of wood. Place the large board on the floor, the side with the two holes in the middle facing up. At each end, place one of the smaller pieces of wood, the sides and ends with three holes lining up to the larger board's three holes, at both ends of the larger board. At one end, place two wooden pegs (hardware b.) in the top and bottom of the three holes, and join the two pieces of wood. Repeat at the other end of the large board.

19. From the end of this assembly, insert a large bolt (hardware i.) into the hole, and a nut (hardware k.) into the hole on the broad part near the end of the long board. Repeat the process of tightening the bolt and nut using a flat head screwdriver and one of the hex keys. Repeat this at the other end of the assembly.

20. Place one flat metal plate (hardware l.) against headboard with the protruding parts at the bottom, lining up the holes in the center close to the bottom of the wood with the top holes in the plate. Screw small screws (hardware h.) into holes, through plate and into headboard. Repeat all on footboard.

21. Hammer all eight metal cylinders (hardware a.) into the four headboard holes and four footboard holes that will face each other.

22. Take the two remaining boards, and place each one in between the headboard and footboard. Be sure to position these boards such that the holes in the boards are facing in with the holes closer to the bottom edge than to the top edge, of the board

when it is in position. With your assistant and you at opposite sides of the footboard, stand it up and fit the metal cylinders in the footboard into the holes in the side boards.

23. Place four large bolts (hardware i.) into holes at foot of headboard, to meet nuts (hardware k.) from inside of side board. Use flat head screwdriver and hex key to tighten the hardware together.

24. Repeat with the headboard what you have done with the footboard: insert cylinders into holes, then four sets of bolts and nuts and tighten.

25. Place the rails (hardware m.) against the side boards. The protruding edge should be on the bottom, the holes against the side board oval in shape. Use eight screws (hardware h.) and a Phillips head screwdriver to secure one rail to one side board. Repeat on other side rail.

26. Take one of the four braces, and lengthen it so that it fits from the plate attached to the headboard, to the round hole on the side rail that on the horizontal part of the rail and nearly halfway to the middle of the bed length.

27. Place the brace so that the top is level with itself, with the end hole lined up with the plate hole but under the plate hole. Insert a tiny screw (hardware f.) through the plate hole and into the brace hole, then tighten with a Phillips head screwdriver.

28. Attach brace to top of side rail by placing brace underneath horizontal part of side rail, placing a tiny screw (hardware f.) on top of the lined up holes, then tightening with a Phillips head screwdriver.

29. Repeat the last two steps three times so that the braces form a diamond in the center of the bed. This diamond's taut-ness should result in the bed being rectangular, as opposed to squeezed in at the middle or bowed in the middle. This tension can be adjusted by either shortening or lengthening the braces.

30. Once you have determined the right tension, find a place in each brace where the opening in one part is over the hole in the other part, put a tiny screw (hardware f.) in that hole and tighten. Repeat on other three braces.

31. Take mid-beam and with its top surface more uniform and longer than its bottom surface, hook it into the plate in the head-board. The hooking action should be such that the mid-beam rests on the plate. Pull the mid-beam towards the center of the footboard. This will lengthen the mid-beam. Hook the mid-beam over the plate that is attached to the footboard.

32. Put eight bolts (hardware g.) through the side rails and mid-beam and tighten them to the eight plastic nuts (hardware e.) Specific holes are: closest to ends of rails, and closest to ends of mid-beams. The holes on the mid-beams are pairs, each pair side by side.

33. Place wood slats on rails and secure first and last rails beyond the four plastic nuts on the rails such that the slats are stretched and will not bunch up.

PROOF

Givens:
- Cliché Field Axiom: A picture is worth a thousand words.
- IKEA TARVA bed assembly instructions are presented in 34 line drawings.
- IKEA TARVA bed assembly instructions are presented in 1829 words (see preceding section of this book).

Nomenclature:
picture (p)
word (w)
line drawing (ld)

Givens:
$p = 1000 \ w$
$1829 \ w = 34 \ ld$

Proof:

$1829 \ w = 34 \ ld$

$1829/34 \ w = 1 \ ld$

$53.8 \ w = 1 \ ld$

$1000 \ w = 1 \ p$

$1000/53.8 = p/ld$

$18.6 = p/ld$

$18.6 \ ld = p$

Therefore, a picture is worth 18.6 line drawings. QED

BALLADE

Brand new designs are here
All with names that will pun
A store that has no peer
In truth, second to none
Always colors that stun
Ingvar K had a good idea
Enjoy free daycare fun
I'm going to IKEA, see ya

There's always a store near
The steepest prices shun
We shop there twice a year
Your worst pricing wars won
You can buy on the run
From Houston clear to the Crimea
Style and chic, not homespun
I'm going to IKEA, see ya

Instructions are so clear
Assembly quickly done
One hour tops, then a beer
Won't you come along, hon
This thing weighs a damn ton
It's my favorite panacea
We'll be home before one
I'm going to IKEA, see ya

Bright yellow sun
Employees kinder than Medea
Cinnamon bun
I'm going to IKEA, see ya

DYSTOPIA

My name is Fern, which means that I am in charge of the ferns
in EA, and also partly in charge of the string instruments. When
I was a baby, the elders looked at me and they could tell that I
should be Fern. At the age of three, like the rest of the children, I
started my education in the dens. The dens are where we learn
the tools we need to exalt Danish furniture design every single
day, in all that we do.

There are many dens, starting at the beginning of the ealphabet,
with the letter e, of course. e-den is where the youngest children
learn skills everybody needs, like reading, writing, and mathematics. Children learn other things in e-den as well, such as
ignoring dreams that invade us by night and by day since they
can make us forget what we know. The children in e-den learn
never walking beyond the wooden wall since there is a danger
of being eaten. There are other important lessons. By the age of
eight, at the very latest, children have finished with e-den.

At the age of nine, depending on the child, children attend
a-den. This is where children are introduced to the most important room in EA, which starts with the letter *A*. This is the room
for working, and it is called the *Atelier*, which means workshop.
It is where the older people in EA spend most of their time, and
do the most important things they ever do. When we say it
out loud, we say At-uh-lee-ay. We learned to read that word in
e-den because it is a word we hear all the time. In a-den, children learn the names of all the woodworking tools. We learn the
planes, the saws, the sharpening tools, felling axe, adz, wedge
and beetle, the square, the clamps, the vices, the mallets, planes,
sanders, miter box, drills, and so many more. My favorite tools
are the gouges: cabinet, bowl, fishtail, paring, firmer, spoon, back
bent, socket and tang. And the similar set of chisels. And all

their sizes and sweeps. We learned about joining, using the fore plane, jointer and strike-block, smoothing plane, rabbet plane and plow.

There is a lot to learn in a-den, and that is why we must learn there until we are twelve, some of us thirteen, if we need a little longer to get everything right. We use all of the tools, making woodworking projects using each tool. Every child must create two hundred and twenty wood projects in the dens. I am a good learner, so I finished my learning in a-den when I was only ten, but that is because I had learned everything in e-den already by the time I was six and a half. Rowan said he was finished with e-den when he was barely six. Rowan is my friend.

After a-den, we learn in b-den. b-den is where we learn about the room that starts with b: bedroom. We learn about sleeping, the importance of rest, about meditation, the circadian rhythm, and other kinds of life cycles. b-den is the first time that boys and girls learn in different rooms. Girls learn about an extra b room. It is called a boudoir. Boys do not learn about the boudoir. When I learned about the boudoir, I was younger than the other girls. The other girls did not want to study with me. It is alright because Rowan is my friend.

I am eleven now, and Rowan is fourteen. I am starting to learn in c-den. Rowan is already learning about Verner Panton in d-den.

When we turn thirteen, or twelve or fourteen or fifteen, depending on our rate of learning, we move our lessons to c-den. This is where we learn about the room that begins with the letter C, the cooking room. We learn about growing and preparing food, and all of the tools we need in the garden and in the cooking room. We start in the garden, learning how to start seeds, plant them and raise plants, and build stakes and trellises. When we learn the cooking room, we make wooden bowls and plates, forks and knives, and spoons of all sizes. It is also in c-den that boys go to another place to learn about another room beginning with the letter C, called the cabinet. I do not know what they learn there, and Rowan never told me.

People are barely children anymore when they learn in d-den, which is when we finally meet the highest form of learning: furniture design. I only know about d-den because Rowan talks about it a lot. Rowan was named after the rowan tree, which is a small tree with clusters of small bright red fruits that look like berries. Rowan's job is to make food from the berries, but his most important job is to know all of the Rowan trees in his orchard. He watches them grow and understands where each trunk and branch grow, how they bend, the health of their branches and leaves. There is only one boy named Rowan in every generation. My friend Rowan, when he is a little bit older, will harvest a rowan tree, and use the wood to make handles and spokes for woodworking tools for all the rest of us. I think that Rowan is *important* because he makes the handle, which is a tool, for all the tools. Rowan says that my view creates a hierarchy and that is wrong, and that his job is just another job, but I cannot help thinking that Rowan was chosen to manage the Rowan orchard and make all of our tool handles because he is smarter than the others.

Studies in d-den begin with the history of furniture making. When it is my time to learn in d-den, my group will hear stories about the oldest, most primitive peoples, their struggles with wood and tools, their achievements and errors. When finally we reach the most current period of history, our studies are broken into five periods, each period corresponding to one main Danish furniture designer. I should explain that "Danish" describes things from the land of Denmark. Before our land was called *EA*, it was called *Denmark*. Some years ago, we threw out all of the consonants in the word Denmark and kept only the vowels, to simplify things.

1. Kaare Klint was the father of Danish furniture design. Before Kaare Klint, there was no furniture at all. People sat on the ground, or on the floor of their houses, or perhaps on stairs or on rocks. While Kaare Klint did not invent the bed, he did invent the table and chair, and all other seating. I think this was twenty-three ages ago. Principles used by Kaare Klint in furniture design included functionality, which means that furniture

is made to be used. Kaare Klint designed furniture for humans, rather than for animals, although sometimes he considered dogs and cats. Kaare Klint changed everything with his furniture. Before his time, people had no time to rest. After he designed the deck chair, somebody had to invent the cruise ship so that his deck chair could be enjoyed appropriately. Similarly, after Kaare Klint invented the safari chair, explorers had to discover Africa and all its animals.

2. Poul Henningsen invented lamps, as well as electricity, and the concept of light in general. His most famous lamp is called simply "PH," though I am not sure why it is not called "a lamp." Poul Henningsen's second most famous lamp is called the artichoke lamp, since it looks like an artichoke. The artichoke lamp is a pendant lamp. Poul Henningsen's other unfortunately overlooked vegetable lamps include the Russet potato lamp and the bok choy lamp.

3. Hans Wegner was a Danish furniture designer who made so many chairs, that by the time he had finished, every person in Denmark had a chair. Others helped Hans Wegner make his chairs, which featured many different designs. After Hans Wegner had designed chairs for all the people in Denmark, he started to design chairs for animals. His peacock chair and his Ox chair stand out as his most successful in this collection. Beyond making chairs for all people in Denmark and for selected animal species, Hans Wegner made two chairs for men named John Fitzgerald Kennedy and Richard Milhous Nixon. It is said that people from all over the world watched these two men talk, disagreeing on many topics while sitting in their Hans Wegner chairs. If people all over the world were able to watch these men have a conversation, they must have been two very large men indeed, and two very large chairs.

4. Finn Juhl designed the "pelican" chair, which seems awfully specific to accommodate one single species of bird. Prior to Hans Wegner's two giant debate chairs, Finn Juhl designed the interior of the Trusteeship Council Chamber at United Nations Headquarters in New York City. I cannot tell from what Rowan says what this means, exactly, but it seems that Finn Juhl was

valued as a person who could design furniture for rooms in which important work was performed, in lands far from Denmark.

5. Verner Panton was most likely insane. We learn that there is probably no other explanation for his cardboard house, given that cardboard is water-soluble. Verner Panton designed a stackable chair, which serves no need since only the top chair in a stack of chairs may be sat upon. The ones underneath just go to waste. Verner Panton also designed a chair made from a failed material called plastic. All in all, Verner Panton had a nearly inexhaustible supply of poor ideas. We also learn that Verner Panton designed a heart chair. Designing a chair for only one human organ is something I am still working on understanding. Rowan does not like to talk about Verner Panton's heart chair, and this is strange since Rowan can explain almost everything else.

After we have finished learning everything in all the dens, we work hard for all the rest of our lives to exalt Danish furniture design every single day, in all that we do. Remember when I told you that Rowan does not like to admit that he is smarter than the others? Well, he really does know that he is capable of more than he reveals. I know this because Rowan and I have a secret. We pretend we are less smart so that we will have time away from the dens to walk in the forest. In the dens we learn that having time that is unstructured is very dangerous, the same as listening to our dreams, the same as falling out of a tree, or being eaten by a wolf. Still, Rowan and I seek this danger. We cannot help ourselves.

One day, Rowan and I were pretending that we could not find twigs for a project whose purpose was to teach the value of indigenous materials that exist all around us. We did this so that we could walk deep in the forest and talk about Danish furniture design, of course. All of a sudden, my eye saw the color blue, which is unexpected on the forest floor. Rowan and I dug into the earth until we exposed a box made of heavy paper containing many small blue papers, each one with identical lettering and lines, each one folded in three. One section of the paper contained lines only, like the notebooks we use in the dens. The papers contained many words that Rowan and I had never seen. They also smelled faintly of fish. We knew this box of papers was very old, from a different world. We told no one, but went back as often as we could to work on understanding what this box of papers meant, to Rowan and me, to EA, and to our purpose: to exalt Danish furniture design every single day, in all that we do.

After about three seasons, a theory of this box of papers emerged from Rowan's and my imaginings. Using a pen he made with Rowan tree wood, and ink he distilled from Rowan tree fruit, Rowan wrote our theory on the bark of birch trees. As we imagined more elements about the past of these blue papers, Rowan wrote and wrote. Rowan stacked all the sheets of birch bark in a deep hole. I culled fern fronds from the acres of ferns that I husband, and lined the hole with them, to protect and preserve these writings.

History of EA
By Rowan and Fern

1. The Box of Papers. We know the box of papers we found in the woods represents aspects of a store called IKEA. Some elements of this paper are: maps of the store showrooms, store marketplace, and store warehouse shelves; store hours; payment methods; store departments; a blank shopping list; special services for delivering, assembling, and installing the furniture sold in the store.

2. The Name IKEA. The store name, IKEA, was an acronym of the store's founder, (Ingvar Kamprad,) his boyhood farm (Elmtaryd,) and his boyhood town (Agunnaryd.)

3. The Book and The Names. By and by, we found a catalogue, which informed us further about IKEA, specifically the names given to all of its products. This naming convention was the key to the demise of IKEA's retail empire and the transformation of Scandinavian society. IKEA named its different furniture divisions after places, lakes, islands and objects. Swedish place names were used for certain types of furnishings, Norwegian place names for others. Danish place names were used for floor coverings, including mats. The ninety-nine cent BOR-RIS map did not attract much attention, since Borris is a small, remote town, however soon after Borris' release came another doormat, this one made of cardboard, priced at forty-nine cents, called KOBENHAVN.

4. Resentments. The cardboard KOBENHAVN mat was only the last straw in a long series of IKEA affronts on the Danish furniture elite. The Danes' resentment of IKEA had been building for many years. When Ingvar Kamprad started IKEA, he met resistance by Swedish furniture makers because of his efficient distribution system, including making a showroom directly above the warehouse, which was a tremendous cost saving. No Swedish furniture makers would sell to IKEA, so Ingvar Kamprad was forced to do business with other countries. He sourced materials from and manufactured in Poland, and sold modern furniture pieces imported from Denmark. At the time, the Danes were the darlings of the furniture world. Mid-century modern was all that there was. But as IKEA succeeded in Scandinavia, and then the rest of Europe, America, Asia, and everywhere, people thought they were buying Swedish design. The Danish designers understood that the design brilliance was theirs alone, and that Ingvar Kamprad was, and always had bee, a brilliant businessman, but never a designer. IKEA headquarters even moved to Humlebaek, Denmark, for many years, but then deserted Denmark for the Netherlands, where IKEA headquarters remained until the Surströmming offensive of 2026. For decades, this tension between Danish design and Swedish industrialism simmered.

5. More Resentments. In 2014, DesignMuseum in Copenhagen mounted an exhibit about Hans Wegner's chairs, opening the week of Hans Wegner's hundredth birthday. This exhibit set in motion the apocalypse that brought about the dystopia we are living in. There were two elements of the exhibit that set things off.

First, on display was a chair from the mid 1940's, called "Peter's chair." This was a chair Hans Wegner made for his friend's son, Peter. He made it in several parts that fit together without nails or glue. The reason he made the chair this was so that he could ship to chair to Peter inexpensively. This was, clearly, the Danes' claim to the invention of IKEA's touted invention, the **flatpack**. Just across the bridge to Sweden and up through Scania, IKEA's corporate culture center exhibited, at the same time, the LÖVET table, the first product it sold in what was *considered a flatpack, over a decade after Peter's Chair.*

Who had really invented the flatpack? Once this dichotomy came to light, in early 2018, the Scandinavian newspapers reported on little else for months. A televised debate between the Danes and the IKEA team was arranged in 2020. The Danish furniture historian chose, naturally, to sit on an original 1949 Hans Wegner "The Chair," to elevate, at least in his mind, the importance of this debate to somewhere in the vicinity of the September 1960 Presidential debate between John F. Kennedy and Richard M. Nixon. Ingvar Kamprad, despite his age, (89,) showed up to the debate with one IVAR chair, ($39.99, solid pine,) still in its flatpack, and proceeded to assemble it during the debate. Few people listened to what was said, but all eyes were on Ingvar. His nimble handling of the hex key impressed international audiences, and IKEA sales shot through the roof. Again.

The case that ended up doing the most to discredit the Danish argument that Hans Wegner had invented the flatpack was contained right in the Hans Wegner exhibit. It turns out that Hans Wegner was studying a Chinese chair c. 1800 when he made Peter's chair. This Chinese chair used no glue or nails, making it possible to assemble once shipped. Once the academic arguments had been published, and the press caught the meaning of this story, the consensus in the furniture world by 2024 was that no designer is ever completely original, and invention is never imagined from nothing. This brought the Danish furniture community down several notches, and that is when the most radical activists among them sprung into action against IKEA.

6. The Surströmming Offensive of 2026. The furious Danish furniture design community produced an enormous quantity of a seasonal Swedish fish product called Surströmming. This product is made from Baltic herring, just prior to spawning. The herring is fermented using lactic acid, producing a pungent smelling fish as well as gases that are barely even containable with advanced canning methods. The angry Danes sent the giftwrapped Surströmming to IKEA Sweden, and when all of the co-workers opened their gifts, the pungent smell plus the effect of the gases rendered every single co-worker unconscious.

7. IKEA Destruction. The Danish furniture activists moved in to the company headquarters and took over everything. They manipulated the

IKEA co-workers emotionally and psychologically until they had transformed the IKEA co-workers into people with no memories, members of a society called EA, which in truth means "IKEA" minus the founder's initials. We have deduced that our society dedicated to the exultation of Danish furniture design exists on the spot that IKEA's first headquarters used to be. We know that the explosion of Surströmming fish gases was so powerful that pieces of furniture and boxes of papers such as the one we found underneath several years of topsoil, flew into the air and were scattered all around the countryside. And that they still smell faintly of fermented fish.

8. EA. People in EA, such as the two of us, Rowan and Fern, are supposed to be shielded from knowledge of any past civilizations, and any civilizations beyond these forests. In reaction to the worldwide fame and fortune brought to IKEA and Sweden by the business practices of Ingvar Kamprad, the Danish furniture community sought to reestablish Danish furniture design as the only inspiration, the only knowledge, and the only furniture future for all persons anywhere.

9. Future. We, Rowan and Fern, understand that knowing EA's true past puts us in danger. We plan to, quietly, and over time, dig a tunnel to Norway. Through this tunnel we will flee. With our deep expertise in furniture making, we will set up a store. We will embrace all of the business principles that the elders of EA have rejected in deference to strictly handcrafted design. We will call our store FREA, an acronym of Fern, Rowan, and EA, the place where we were born, where we learned, and where we came to realize we had to leave. One day we will return. We will open a branch of our store here, where Ingvar Kamprad started it all. We believe that ideas and design belong to all, and that all can enjoy it, either in its purest form, or diluted, disassembled, and distributed all over the world. Our store will bring these principles back- reestablish 3D design: diluted, disassembled, and distributed. We will call our store FREA, but we will pronounce it "free."

GLOSSARY OF WRITING STYLES/GENRES

(in order of appearance)

COPYRIGHT

A copyright notice informs readers of the underlying claim to copyright ownership in a published work, thereby acting as a deterrent to theft.

ACKNOWLEDGEMENTS

Authors state their appreciation for people, or food items, that contributed positively to the creation of the work.

INTRODUCTION

I read somewhere, sometime, that a book's introduction is like the entrance hall of the book- definitely part of the book, as opposed to being outside of the book. An *intro*, as we say in the book *biz*, is not a foreword, since a foreword is written by a person other than the author. Attempting to stick with our architecture analogy, a foreword is like the small structure at the gate of the property, in which much manpower is spent to clear people for entrance. A foreword usually makes the book seem more important and more valid, and worth its usually higher price. An introduction is not a preface, since the preface often includes material included in the acknowledgements section, which definitely comes from the author, but is outside of the book. Both a preface and an introduction may justify the book's existence and explain why it was written. A preface is a literary entrance hall with lots of thank you notes in the outgoing mail tray.

SONNET

A sonnet is a poetic form originating in Italy in the thirteenth century. My sonnet is Shakespearian, which means it is written in iambic pentameter, and contains the rhyme scheme **abab, cdcd, efef, gg**. *Iambic pentameter* means that each line contains ten syllables, with emphasis on the even numbered syllables. Pentameter means "measuring five," and corresponds to five units of sound. An iamb is a sound sequence, a short sound followed by a longer sound, as in the word "dismay." The two sounds of an iamb multiplied by the five units of the pentameter produce ten syllables per line. The sonnet's fourteen lines multiplied by ten syllables per line produce a poem of one hundred and forty syllables. *Caution:* when the word "iamb" is capitalized, it may be erroneously pronounced, "lamb," as in a baby sheep. While lamb imagery does figure in the critical interpretation of poetry more often than other farm animals do, please use caution when capitalizing "iamb."

LEGEND

A legend is a narrative account of events. Its truth lies somewhere between a chronicle, which emphasizes fact, and myth, which emphasizes symbolic meaning. Legends are usually potentially true, but not always expected to be true.

ANTHEM

An anthem is a song representing an organization, usually a country. I see no reason not to give a store an anthem.

COMPLAINT

I can't believe I have to explain this word. What a chore. I don't have enough hours in the day to write this. Why can't people look up words themselves? I wish I did not have to explain this word. (That was I complaining.)

PRODUCT RECALL

When a manufacturer or a store that sells a product learns that it is unsafe, frequently the product will be recalled, which means that an announcement is made and publicized, and customers are urged to stop using the product and return it for a full refund.

QUATRAIN

A quatrain is a poem of four lines. There are several more or less common rhyme schemes, but one of the most common and the one in this book is the *abab* rhyme scheme.

FORMULA

A formula is an expression of a chemical, mathematical, or geometrical truth. In this book, the formula expresses the numbers needed for and used to calculate the required quantity of fabric for a certain task.

D.I.Y. INSTRUCTIONS

D.I.Y. means "Do It Yourself." Instructions are steps in performing a given task. "D.I.Y. Instructions" is therefore somewhat of a redundant expression, since instructions imply that you are doing something, making the "Do It Yourself" part of the title unnecessary. On the other hand, without the inclusion of the "D.I.Y.," the instructions could read, "Don't make the desired thing. Buy it."

FAIRY TALE

A fairy tale is a story usually featuring fairies, ghosts, trolls or other beasts, in which characters possess the ability to perform magic or have other unrealistic faculties. Another meaning of a fairy tale has come to be the "fairy tale ending" in which the characters, at least the good ones, live "happily ever after." And by "good," the fairy tale interpreters means the characters on moral high ground. *Happily ever after* includes death or a prison life sentence for wrongdoers of all stripes.

WARNING LABEL

Warning labels appear on a great number of products, and their incidence is increasing. Filing lawsuits against companies for failing to warn people against every conceivable risky action while anywhere near the product in question, is clearly on the rise. This makes me feel that in order to be "on trend" in the legal sense, I must warn you: Do not read this book while operating a motor vehicle, while cooking, or while chopping wood. This list of activities that are incompatible with reading this book is by no means complete. For a complete list of activities incompatible with reading this book, please include every verb, except for: sitting, breathing, and reading.

MYSTERY

A mystery, when referring to a written story, often means a story in which a detective or other clever character, works to uncover clues, posits a hypothesis, performs a statistically reliable, three year, double-blind clinical trial, publishes his or her results in a refereed journal, and only then claims to know whodunnit. Detectives are often street smart and intuitive, making it nearly impossible for the reader to figure out the solution before the detective. In my story, my detective character knew whodunnit three pages before I did.

FLOW CHART

A flow chart is a graphic representation of a causal sequence of events or stages in a process.

SESTINA

A sestina is a wickedly complicated poem. I don't know how old this poetic form is, or where it is from, and I am not going to look it up because I am still plenty resentful about the time I invested in writing one. Here is how a sestina works: You write a six-line stanza. None of the words have to rhyme, and the meter is not so important. So far so good, you are thinking. But wait. The fun is already over, because the rest of the sestina is like solving a New York Times Saturday Crossword Puzzle with half the clues missing. Let us say the last "words" of your first stanza are "123456." That means the last words of the next stanza are "615243." See the pattern? The pattern for determining the last word of the next stanza is: last/first/second to last/ second/third to last/third. Your third stanza's six last words are "364125." And you write six stanzas like that. And if that's not enough, after those thirty-six lines, you write the *envoi*, which is three lines, each line split into two parts, the last word of each of the six parts being "621453." Writing sestinas is for people who like balancing stoichiometric equations, and for show-offs.

OBITUARY

An obituary is a death notice, and more. Obituaries often include a narrative of the deceased's life, featuring achievements, a list of surviving relatives, time and place of funeral services, and where to send charitable donations in lieu of flowers.

NURSERY RHYME

A nursery rhyme is a poem or song intended for young children (in nurseries). They often have some kind of moral message, but are just as often to make babies giggle or to lull them to sleep.

ICELANDIC SAGA

The Icelandic sagas are narratives, recounting the movements and genealogy of Icelandic families. Dating from the medieval period, the sagas tell of many ships sailed and terrain worked, in dry chronicle form. The sagas are, let's say, not exactly models of currently marketable story structure.

ACRONYM AND ANAGRAMS

An acronym is a series of letters, each letter standing in for an entire word. An anagram is a word or phrase constructed from the letters of another word or phrase, often expressing similar or ironically different meanings, "This anagram" <=> "A mashing art"

STREAM OF CONSCIOUSNESS

Stream of consciousness is a narrative form that depicts the narrator's interior monologue, or loose amalgamation of thoughts.

COUPLET

A couplet is a two-line rhyme
To write a poor one takes little time

RECIPE

A recipe is, in a way, the same as a set of D.I.Y. instructions, but specifically for food preparation. Also, by convention, a recipe begins with a list of ingredients needed for the food preparation. Recipes rarely list the hardware needed to complete the instructions. Fortunately, sometimes the title of the recipe gives us a clue. For example, when a recipe title includes the term "Oven Roasted," that is a clue that you will need an oven to successfully complete the recipe. Moreover, you might infer that you will also need a roasting pan, and electricity or gas or some other energy source to power your oven. The recipe also never mentions all the dishes you will have to clean after completing the steps, so it is best to factor that time in to the often-misleading "Prep Time and Cooking Time."

HELP WANTED AD

Job Ad, Job Posting, Employment Advertisement.

LIMERICK

Limerick is a city in western Ireland, on the River Shannon. It is also a poetic form of five lines with rhyme scheme aabba, and syllables usually numbering 8-*8-5-5-8* or *9-9-5-5-9*. Limericks are supposed to be humorous and traditionally are obscene.

SOCRATIC DIALOGUE

A Socratic dialogue is a dialogue among several speakers, dating from Classical Greece, most written by Plato. Each dialogue is a discussion of moral and philosophical principles. The most renowned Socratic dialogues include *Republic, Phaedo,* and *Symposium*. The dialogue *Cratylus* concerns the nature of names and features one character called Cratylus, as well as Socrates and a philosopher named Hermogenes.

CONVENTION

There are several meanings of *Convention*, however in terms of a writing genre, it is a set of generally agreed upon procedures or principles of practice.

TRIOLET

A triolet is a poem of eight lines, written in iambic tetrameter, dating from a long long time ago in France. The rhyming scheme of a triolet is ABaAabAB, where the letter A is a line that rhymes with the line a, and is identical to other lines called A. Likewise, a line called B rhymes with the line called b, and is identical to the line called B at the end. This means there are two words that rhyme with the last word of line A, and one word that rhymes with the last word of line B. (For a definition of *iamb,* see SONNET.) Tetrameter means four sections of meter. Since iambs have two syllables each, iambic tetrameter contains eight syllables, and the entire poem contains sixty-four syllables. For a total of only sixty-four syllables, all these rules hardly seem worth the effort.

SHOPPING LIST

Have you ever made a list of items to buy before a trip to the grocery store? Most of us have.

AUTOBIOGRAPHY

It is interesting that an autobiography is a biography written or told by the person whose life is being recounted, and not the biography of a car. We have come to use the whole word *auto* to mean car, whereas the prefix *auto-* means self. We have come to identify so essentially with our cars, that perhaps every autobiography ought to include all cars owned by the subject, as well as all of the subject's car-related experiences.

RONDEAU CINQUAIN

Rondeau cinquain. Here we have another medieval French poetry form with plenty of rhymes and repeats. And, the rondeau is not one poetic form, but three, presenting us with options: Rondeau simple (8 lines, same as a triolet,) Rondeau tercet (13 lines,)

Rondeau quatrain (16 lines,) and the big cheese of the Rondeau family, Rondeau cinquain (21 lines). The Rondeau cinquain has five sections. The first and last sections are called the refrain, and are five lines each, characterized by rhyme scheme *aabba*. The middle (third) section of the Rondeau cinquain is the first three lines of the refrain. So, once you have written five lines, you already have thirteen of twenty-one lines done. The second section contains three lines, the first two rhyming with a and the third rhyming with b, or, essentially rhyming with the third section, line for line. The fourth section contains five lines and rhymes, line for line, with the refrain: *aabba*. With all this repetition, a rondeau seems more like a song than a poem. This makes sense since rondeaus were often set to music. I have set mine to music for soprano voice, and added alto, tenor and bass parts so that nobody feels left out or gets bored and goes out back and takes up cigarette smoking.

VILLANELLE

Villanelle is a beautiful poetic form. If you know Dylan Thomas' poem *Do Not Go Gentle into That Good Night*, you know a villanelle.

> *Do not go gentle into that good night,*
>
> *Old age should burn and rave at close of day;*
>
> *Rage, rage against the dying of the light.*

These are the first three lines of the poem. The first line (A1) is one line of the "refrain" and the third line (A2) is the second line of the "refrain" but these two lines do not appear one after the other until they appear as the very last two lines of the poem. The villanelle is very repetitive, following the rhyme scheme *A1-b-A2/a-b-A1/a-b-A2/a-b-A1/a-b-A2/a-b-A1-A2*. Unlike a song with more straightforward repetitions, the villanelle plays with the lines of the refrain in what feels like compulsion.

PLAY

To play is a verb. To play a story is to have people enact characters in a story, on a stage, with an audience. *A play*, the noun, is the written work intended for this portrayal.

FABLE

A fable is a fictional story featuring anthropomorphized animals or other normally non-speaking creatures. Fables are intended to communicate aspects of the human condition, often stating their moral at the conclusion of the action.

ODE

An ode is a poem written in praise of something. John Keats' *Ode on a Grecian Urn* is perhaps the best-known example. An English ode usually follows the rhyme scheme ***abab, cde, cde***. Like *Ode on a Grecian Urn*, my ode is written in iambic pentameter [see SONNET].

COMPARISON

Jimmy is taller than Kevin. Kevin is brighter than Larry. Larry looks more appealing than Ed. Ed is luckier than Jimmy. These are direct comparisons of fictitious boys' attributes [see NARRATIVE NON-FICTION for comments on whether these boys are really fictitious.] Notice how these comparisons become less and less objective from first to last. When comparing apples to oranges, be sure to note that both are fruit, in order to make your comparison seem more useful than it might otherwise be.

FAN FICTION

A relatively new development, fan fiction is fictional stories using the characters and fictional world of another author's work.

The writer is supposedly a fan of the original author's work (or a calculating scoundrel). Another property of fan fiction is that it is that, at least in the United States of America, rights to it are protected under copyright law, belonging to the original author. Fan fiction rights are derivative rights that can be sold, just like movie rights, or action figure rights. This is why fan fiction is free all over the internet, and fan fiction has never, ever been thinly veiled and sold for money without the original author's permission. Exceptions are of course when the original work is in the public domain, which is when there is no copyright holder on the original work.

EPISTLE

An epistle is a letter, usually a formal letter, usually an open letter, to a group of people. Epistles include Pauline letters and letters from Apostles to Christians. The reason the words epistle and apostle sound similar is because they both derive from Greek, both from words meaning messenger/letter. If you think about it, a letter and a messenger are the same thing, except that one is a person who speaks a message and one is a message of words on paper.

TERZA RIMA

Terza Rima is a rhyme scheme of interlocking stanzas: *aba, bcb, cdc, ded*, etc. (etc is not a stanza.) The end of a terza rima poem is either one more or two more lines of the middle rhyme of the last three-line stanza. Therefore, the above example might end either *ded e*, or *ded ee*. Dante Alighieri wrote his Divine Comedy in terza rima verse.

DIARY ENTRY

Dear Diary,
Today I defined "diary entry" and other terms for my book about IKEA. I also ate quite a lot of chocolate. Diary, you are the

only one who understands me, which is troubling since you are basically a stack of papers. On the other hand, you are way more interactive than a lot of therapists, and easier on the pocketbook.

SPORTS COMMENTARY

Sports commentary may be more of a verbal form than a written form. We non-broadcasters do not know how much commentary is fed to the broadcasters on teleprompters. There do seem to be a lot of prepared "offhand" remarks in certain broadcast sports. We certainly hope the play by play is ad libbed. After all, if any announcer should be prepared for a curveball in the action, it is a sports commentator.

OCTAVE

An octave is an eight-line poem in iambic pentameter [see SON-NET] following rhyme scheme **abba abba**.

PHILOSOPHY

A philosophy is one or more basic concepts that guide the conduct and thought of a particular person or group. Philosophies can be as general as those concerning existence, or specific to a business practice, for example.

NARRATIVE NON-FICTION

Narrative non-fiction is a story, like fiction, but unlike fiction, the story is true. This begs the question of truth in fiction. Not everything in a work of fiction is untrue. For example, most fiction is written in a world where gravity exists, and people breathe in oxygen and breathe out carbon dioxide. At least we assume these things go on, otherwise they probably would be noted as fictional aspects of the story, being highly inconvenient. Conversely, non-fiction assumes that everything in the story is true. If my story refers to a man named Bob, and his name is actually Bill, does that make my entire story a work of fiction? At what point, meaning after how many approximations or lies, does non-fiction become fiction? Moreover, if a fictional story is entirely possible, then how does the author know it has not actually happened, say, in a different city, or at a different period of history? How do we know what is fiction and what is non-fiction? I cannot answer these questions, but I can attest to the fact that my brief piece of narrative non-fiction is in fact all fact, at least in my mind. There is a possibility that I have made some errors of fact, but these are entirely unintentional. I am not sure such errors would make my narrative non-fiction into fiction. I do not think they would. *[Discuss at your next book group.]*

HAIKU

Traditional Japanese haiku poetry is written in one seventeen-syllable verse, the syllables divided into three lines of **5-7-5** syllables each. Traditional haiku are most often written about elements in nature.

TANKA

Tanka are traditional Japanese poems of thirty-one syllables each. They are composed of an upper phrase, which is the same as a haiku in length and structure, and a lower phrase, which is two lines of seven syllables each. The resulting tanka verse is **5-7-5-7-7**. The middle line is a pivot line, uniting the first part and last part of the poem.

ASSEMBLY INSTRUCTIONS

There is often more than one way to assemble a piece of furniture from its parts. Some people enjoy figuring it out as they go along, but most do not. In the interest of sanity, time management, and business sense, assembly instructions are packaged with almost every product requiring assembly of any kind.

PROOF

How do we move from hypothesis to certainty, from question to reliable answer? The answer is a proof. Using logic and basic axioms and assumptions, we build on what we know, until we can be sure that we know something that before we built the proof we did not know, or at least were not sure we knew. What can be made more certain using a proof? Not as much as we thought. Not even geometrical proofs are absolutely reliable. For about two thousand years, it appeared as though parallel lines never met in space. Turns out, they do. So all those rectangles and triangles with lettered sides and angles that you fiddled with until you think you learned something were mirages, in the end as uncertain as which card is the queen in Three Card Monte. What turns out to be the key in any proof is the definition of the universe. Does a rectangle have parallel lines in space all the way to infinity? No. Does a rectangle have parallel lines in the universe of my weekend project of building a bench? Yes.

BALLADE

A ballade is different from a ballad. A ballade is a form of French poetry, often set to music, dating from over a thousand years ago. A ballade's structure is three eight-line stanzas, each with the rhyme scheme *ababbcbC*, where *C* is an identical line in each stanza (a sort of refrain). After the three stanzas, the ballade ends with four lines of rhyme scheme *bcbC*, again with the same last line *C*.

DYSTOPIA

Dystopia fiction is fiction about a society or community or world that is undesirable as a result of humanity having gone down the wrong path, at least compared to what we are used to. A dystopia novel commonly contains the following elements: set in the future, often after some kind of partial apocalypse that spares only a subset of humanity; a tyrannical government; brainwashed masses; the secret preservation of some pre-dystopic element, which acts as the only hope of overthrowing the dystopia and restoring the world, or the community, to its previous, or even preferable to its previous equilibrium.

11395325R00079

Printed in Great Britain
by Amazon